MW00614277

The A to Z
of Whisky
Place-Names:
Landscape,
Language &
Invention

Jacob King

Whittles Publishing

Whittles Publishing Ltd.,
Dunbeath,
Caithness, KW6 6EG,
Scotland, UK

www.whittlespublishing.com

© 2022 Jacob King

ISBN 978-184995-503-4

All rights reserved.
No part of this publication may be reproduced,
stored in a retrieval system, or transmitted,
in any form or by any means, electronic,
mechanical, recording or otherwise
without prior permission of the publishers.

Printed in the UK by Cambrian Printers Ltd

Contents

Preface

As part of my work for *Ainmean-Àite na h-Alba*, for several years an event was run during the Edinburgh Gaelic Week with the Water of Life Society, the whisky society of the University of Edinburgh. Five whiskies were discussed; someone from the society talked about each whisky and I spoke about the name of the whisky as it applied to a place-name.

The level of interest in this topic surprised me, but what astounded me more was that there was no scholarly complete work on the subject. Most studies had been done as quirky articles in magazines and the same folk-etymologies about names tended to have been recirculated with no fact-checking.

This book began with the research I did for those events, and then included work I have undertaken for my professional toponymic research. When I started this project, I did not expect there to be so many place-names, nor was I aware of how many 'fake' names there were on whisky bottles. It soon became clear to me that there was a book's worth of material.

Acknowledgements

Thanks goes to the following people and organisations: Ainmean Àite na h-Alba, specifically Eilidh Scammell; The Scotch Malt Whisky Society, Neil Aitken and Mads Schmoll; The University of Edinburgh: Bria Mason, Gaelic Officer; The Water of Life Society, the Centre for Research Collections; Sabhal Mòr Ostaig: Dr Dòmhnall Uilleam Stiùbhart; The National Library of Scotland; Jo NicDhòmhnaill, Prof. Richard Cox, Dr Simon Taylor, Ian Fraser, Dr Guto Rhys, Dr Peadar Morgan and my wife, family and parents for all their support and patience.

Introduction
What this book is and what it is not

This is not a book about Scotch whisky; rather, this is a book about the origin, development and meaning of place-names found on whisky bottles. Such a name can be the name of the whisky or the name of the distillery, broadly speaking. As such, this book is not concerned with whisky itself except where it pertains to the place-name.

This book, therefore, is about place-names. In deciding which place-names should be included in the book, one of the following is applicable: if the distillery has been open after 1950; if the site of the distillery is visible today, or if the place-name appears in writing on a whisky bottle one could reasonably buy.

Some place-names discussed in this book go back two thousand years, whereas some were invented wholesale in the twenty-first century. Many of the names incorporate earlier names but have added elements or changed the spelling for various reasons.

There are thousands of limited bottlings numbering only a few hundred or so bottles, particularly miniatures, and this book cannot claim to include all of these. Moreover, there have – over the centuries – been many small distilleries in Scotland, not all of which were legal, and this book does not include every single one of these.

Place-names are not always what they seem

The study of place-names or 'toponymy' is a complex discipline that has many unexpected twists and turns. Unfortunately, many place-name explanations online and in books about Scotch whisky are inaccurate or merely repeat advertisers' marketing spin. In this book, I have aimed to ignore previously offered derivations and to take nothing for granted.

The study of toponymy is especially difficult in Scotland where the vast majority of place-names do not derive from the dominant language of the twenty-first century, which is English. With that in mind, it is useful to take a few points into account. These points stand not just for Scotland but the whole world.

The high register word for the study of place-names is toponymy, and the study of names, in general, is onomastics. While it might not be correct to call the study of names a full-blown 'science', the study of place-names is nonetheless a discipline with its own methods and types of evidence. This is another way of stating that we cannot simply decide on a place-name derivation off the top of our head and claim that to be the truth, even if we have lived in that place all one's life, or if we speak the same language from which we think the place-name derives.

When we want to research a place-name, we should gather as many written early forms of the name as possible. When put in chronological order, this can show us how the name has evolved. As this is a popular book, I have endeavoured only to add a single early form for each place-name discussed, where possible. If there is none mentioned, it means none exists before the nineteenth-century Ordnance Survey records.

Another important piece of evidence is how the name is or was pronounced. Where a place-name does not have an obvious pronunciation to an English speaker, I have added in a rudimentary guide.

A thorough knowledge of the languages from which the name could come is also needed. By this, I do not simply mean fluency in the language, but an awareness of its historical development, given that, if the place-name is old, it will have been coined in an earlier form of the language than the one spoken today. This is another way of saying that just because we speak a language it does not make us experts in it.

Humans are naturally drawn to narrative: stories that make sense of the world. This is a very good thing, but often when it comes to the study of place-names, people prefer a good story rather than the more usual prosaic truth of a matter. To give an example, the northern part of Scotland is called Sutherland. One story says this comes from someone who was shipwrecked off its coast and upon seeing it said in Scots 'Soo, there land'! A good story, but not much else. The name Sutherland comes from the Old Norse *suðrland* meaning 'south land', from the Vikings' perspective. For examples of other names that do not look like what they seem, see Ryelaw and Aultmore.

The Languages of Scotland

With one possible exception, all the known indigenous languages in Scotland are what modern scholars call Indo-European. This describes a theoretical reconstructed language that is the 'mother' of nearly all European languages. In Scotland, all languages derive from two intermediate reconstructed 'proto-languages' which we call proto-Celtic and proto-Germanic.

Proto-Celtic or Old Celtic is a theoretical language that has been reconstructed based on linguistic evidence, we have very little direct evidence of it. Over time, this evolved into its living descendants. The surviving spoken Celtic languages are Scottish Gaelic, in use in Scotland and Canada; Irish in Ireland; Manx on the Isle of Man; Welsh in Wales and Patagonia; Breton in France and Cornish in Cornwall.

Proto-Germanic divided over time and gave birth to many languages labelled Germanic. Some of them are: English, Scots, German and the Scandinavian languages – Swedish, Danish, and Norwegian (also referred to as Norse or Viking). There seems to be a common belief that English derives from Latin, but it does not, it has merely borrowed many loanwords from that language.

Old Celtic

Names of the larger islands and longer rivers are some of the oldest names in Scotland and some of these do not fit any identifiable language. Other names are likely from a Celtic language, but which individual one is not known. All these names have been bunched together into the heading Old Celtic, but it should be made clear this is a largely reconstructed language, and the meanings and forms offered are theoretical.

Pictish / British / Brittonic / Cumbric

All the names above refer to Celtic languages which are no longer extant in Scotland, but whose closest living relative is Welsh. Aside from some inscriptions, the only way we know about this language is through place-names themselves. Unfortunately, this means there are vast parts of the language that we know nothing or very little about. We are not even sure about the differences between the languages mentioned above. They were possibly different dialects of the same language.

We know very little about the arrival of the Celtic languages to the British Isles, but there was presumably linguistic migration from antiquity up into the historical era. Apart from some hard-to-decipher old place-names, some sort of Celtic language is the earliest languages we know of that must have been spoken in what we now call Scotland (and indeed the British Isles). This language (or languages) evolved into the languages mentioned above. In Scotland, Pictish was likely spoken throughout most of modern Scotland, except perhaps for southern Argyll. We do not know if it was spoken in the Outer Hebrides, Shetland or Orkney, however.

The Pictish language and culture began to give way to the new fashionable Gaelic language from around AD 800 and it was most likely functionally extinct by the tenth century AD.

Gaelic

Modern research has rewritten the story of if and how Gaelic came to Scotland, and that story is still changing at the time of writing. Traditional history tells us that Gaelic was first spoken in Ireland and was brought across with the Kingdom of the Dal Riata in AD 500. The real picture, however, was probably more complicated than this, with parts of Argyll perhaps having been Gaelic-speaking for as long as Ireland. We do know, however, that Gaelic encroached from the south-west up through Scotland as far as Caithness in the north, to the Hebrides and as far south as Galloway and the Borders. The maximum extent of Gaelic was likely round about the twelfth century. Since then, the language has faced a slow decline in speakers, accelerating in the twentieth century. This has been due to several factors, including the eighteenth- and nineteenth-century Clearances that evacuated people from their traditional land. There was, moreover, a prevailing view amongst some Lowlanders that Gaelic was a barbarous language that would be better stamped out, this was called in Gaelic *Mi-rùn nan Gall* 'the hatred of the Lowlanders'; unfortunately, this attitude still exists today.

The Isle of Man is an island between Ireland and the north of England, and it has its own type of Gaelic called Manx, which is distinct from both Scottish Gaelic and Irish, especially in its spelling system, which is completely different.

Norse

Driven by population pressures in Scandinavia, Vikings first started to raid the coast of Scotland and the rest of the British Isles around AD 800. Eventually, these seafaring peoples settled around the coastal areas. They seemed to have intermarried with the local Gaelic population, and after a period of bilingualism, the Norse language ceased to be spoken in Scotland but it left behind it many place-names and words in Gaelic. Although people think now of the Western Isles as a bastion of the Gaelic language, a look at the place-names will reveal that the vast majority of the names of settlements and larger natural features are from Norse, such as Bhaltos from Norse *Vatnlausa* 'waterless place'. Likewise, many words in Gaelic, especially those to do with marine life, come originally from Norse, such as *acair* 'anchor' or *sgioba* 'staff'.

Scots

Scots and English are both Germanic languages, sharing the same mother language, Old English. Scots should not be confused with Scottish Gaelic which is a Celtic language. Old English first came to be spoken in the British Isles from about the sixth century AD. This language broke into various dialects and reached the south of Scotland about the time of David I (1124–53). Thereafter Scots slowly encroached into previously Gaelic-speaking areas, aided by the foundation of burghs in Scotland.

Scots became the dominant language of the Lowlands from around the fourteenth century up until the modern era. It was used for legal charters after Latin fell out of fashion. From around the Union in 1603, Scots began to become slowly anglicised, which means it came under the influence from the separate, but similar, language of English. Over time, Scots became diluted and more like English until it turned into Standard Scottish English or the 'Scottish accent'. Unfortunately, Scots is often seen as a 'low status' language or dialect these days. This was not always the case, and there is a large body of Scots literature by the likes of Robert Louis Stevenson and Robert Burns, as well as legal texts.

English

English is a relatively late newcomer to Scotland, at the expense of both Gaelic and Scots. Today, it is the *lingua franca* of the whole of Scotland.

The Ebb and Flow of Languages

It is important to remember that every living language evolves. This means that a language spoken at one time may become unintelligible to a speaker a few hundred years older. All of these languages discussed above have changed over time; some have split into different languages, others have died off, and all have borrowed words from other languages and incorporated them into their own. There is no such thing as a 'pure' form of a language.

No language or culture exists in a vacuum; this observation is especially true when considering Scottish place-names. The name Pittentrail in Sutherland is an excellent example of a name that shows influence from all of Scotland's languages.

Pett was a Pictish word borrowed into Gaelic meaning 'farmstead', and it was used for a time by Gaels in the construction of new names after Pictish had ceased to be spoken in Scotland. The Gaels also borrowed words from the Norse people, especially terms to do with the sea. One of these words was Norse *Þræll* 'slave' (think of the English word 'thrall', or 'enthralled') which came into Gaelic as *tràill*. The Gaels then coined the name for a farm, using Gaelic words, albeit borrowed from other languages, they called it Peit an Tràill 'the farmstead of the slave'; perhaps a freed slave had first settled there. Gaels became bilingual again, this time speaking Gaelic and Scots, this name was then pronounced naturally in Scots as Pittentraill, although, as with us, the meaning was unknown to monolingual Scots speakers. The picture is further complicated by the fact that at this time the Gaelic word *peit* became unfashionable and was substituted for the more popular Gaelic word *baile* also meaning 'farm or town'. Thus today, whilst the English is Pittentrail, the Gaelic is Baile an Tràill.

Thus, it is important to bear in mind that Pittentraill is, nonetheless, a Gaelic name, despite the origin of the words within the name. In the same way, one would not say that a name such as Prince's Street in Edinburgh was Latin in origin because the words within it come from Latin *princeps* and *strātum* respectively.

Pronunciation Guide

A pronunciation guide has been given in square brackets for names whose pronunciation is not obvious to the average English speaker. Gaelic and Scots have many sounds that do not exist in most varieties in English; therefore, the guide below is necessarily approximate. For those who are familiar with the International Phonetic Alphabet (IPA), the appropriate symbol has been included in square brackets. Underline denotes where the syllable is stressed.

gh [ɣ] a voiced guttural sound, the same as the g in German *tag*.

x [χ] a voiceless guttural sound, most famously heard in the Scots word *loch*.

c [ç] a voiceless guttural sound, pronounced as in *ich* in German.

ky [c] a voiceless palatal stop.

dh [ð] voiced *th* as in 'the'.

th [θ] voiceless *th* as in 'theory'.

g [g] is always hard.

ñ [ɲ] is a palatal n, which is the same as the first n heard in the Spanish word *mañana*.

N [ṉ] a dental n. This sound does not exist in English.

L [L] a 'dark' l as heard in Russian. This sound does not exist in English but it is close to the final sound in [all].

Ĩ [ʎ] a slender l which does not exist in English.

tch [tʃ] as in *watch*

j represents [dʲ] in Gaelic, [dʒ] in English.

In Gaelic, many consonants are pronounced somewhat differently from English, and the above system cannot represent all these, but t, d and n are pronounced, broadly speaking as dentals ([ṉ], [ḏ], [ṉ]). Likewise, r can represent [rʲ], [ɾ] or even [ð]; [k] can represent [kʲ] or [k] or [kʰ];

ə [ə] is the unstressed vowel as heard in *the*.

e [ɛ] as in *egg*

o [o] as in *got*

au [aʊ] as in *mouse*

aa [ɑ:] a long a which is a sound that does not exist in English.

oo [o:] a long o sound, somewhat like the o in more, not oo as in book or hoot.

ei [ei] approximating *play*

ai [ɑi] i as in *mile*

uu [uː] as in *doom*

u [ʊ] as in *pull*

i [ɪ] as in *pit*

ii [iː] a longer version of the above sound

w [ɯ] a sound as heard in curl, but without the -r-.

ʌ [ʌ] u as in muck

A tilde over a vowel represents that it is nasalised, e.g. [õ].

Scottish place-names are notoriously difficult to pronounce to the uninitiated. A whole book could be written about how to pronounce them, but the following guidelines will be of some help.

In names of Gaelic origin, the stress often lies on the second less familiar element. Thus, if a name begins with any number of familiar elements, such as Bal- (Bal<u>more</u>), Ach- or Auch- (Auch<u>rann</u>ie), Inver- (Inver<u>ness</u>), Aber- (Aber<u>milk</u>), Kil(l)- (Kil<u>don</u>an), the stress or accent will generally fall on the first syllable after it. An exception to this will be for the syllable -en- (e.g. Balen<u>don</u>ich) where the stress will fall after this. (This -en- normally represents the definite article meaning 'of the').

For place-names with two syllables ending in -aig, the stress generally lies on the first syllable, and the last syllable is pronounced -ig or -ik, not -ayg. For example, Mallaig is [<u>ma</u>lik] or [<u>ma</u>lig] not [ma<u>layg</u>].

More often than not, -ch- is pronounced as -x-, not as tch as in 'watch', unless it stands at the start of the word or appears in a word you already recognise. For example, Charing Cross has -tch-, but Auchrannie has an -x-.

-lz- comes from an Old Scots palatal -l- sound, and usually, will be pronounced either as an -l- or as a -y-, but never as an actual l followed by a z. Thus, Culzean as [kullain] and Dalziel as [dii-el]. Likewise -nz- is usually pronounced as -ñ-, thus Binzian is pronounced [biñən].

Pronunciations throughout this book have only been offered for modern forms in living languages. The historical pronunciations of names in languages which are no longer extant in Scotland brings with it issues which fall outside the scope of this book.

Maps

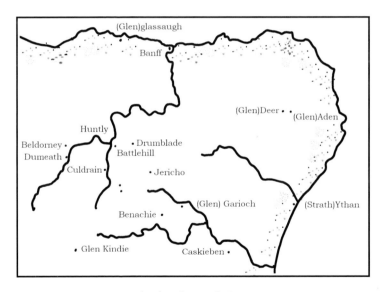

Aberdeenshire and Moray

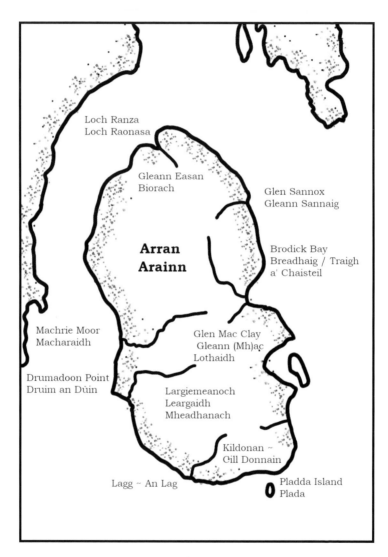

Arran

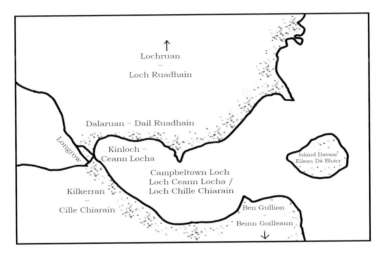

Campbeltown

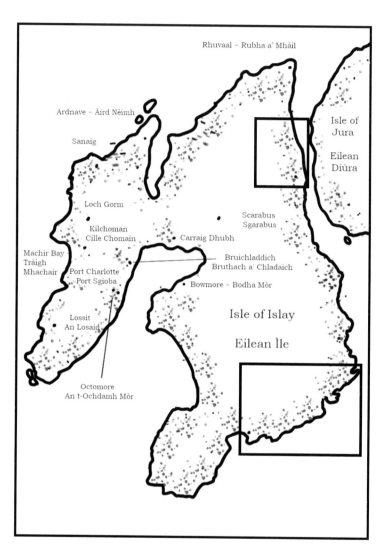

Isle of Islay. See next page for insets.

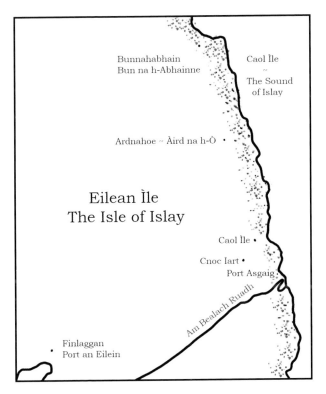

The Isle of Islay and the Sound of Islay

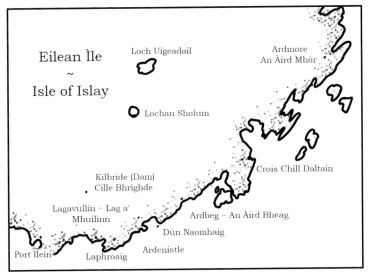

The Isle of Islay – South coast

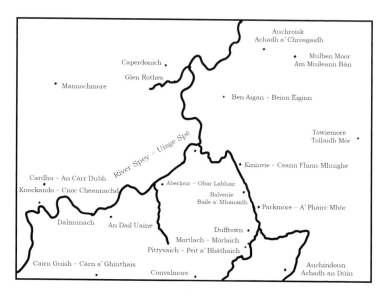

Speyside – North

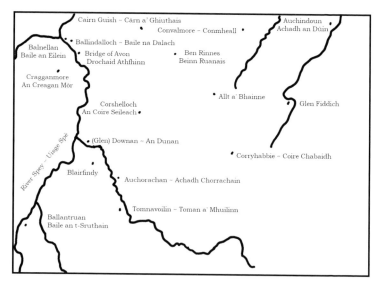

Speyside – South

The Place-Names

Aberargie

Perthshire (*Apurfeirt* in the tenth century) [abər argi]

Aberargie is a name of Pictish origin meaning 'the mouth of the River Farg'. The first element is *aber* 'confluence' (discussed below) which is followed by a form of the River Farg or Fargie. This element comes from a Pictish word which also exists in Gaelic, as *fearg* 'angry' and probably relates to the way the river flows; *fearg* can also mean a 'warrior', so possibly the name relates to the river's metaphorical 'warlike' manner. The -f- is not pronounced in the modern form due to Gaelic syntax, hence the reason the name is not *Aberfargie. In modern Gaelic, the name is Obar Fheargaidh [opər ereki]. Farragon Hill in Perthshire is in Gaelic Feargan [ferekan] using the same root.

ABERS AND INVERS

There are many place-names in Scotland beginning with Aber- and Inver-; the places they represent normally sit at the foot of a river or burn, whilst the second element is – more often than not – the name of that watercourse. Although deriving from different languages, both these words once meant 'confluence', 'inlet', or 'river-foot'. Aber- is a Pictish word, deriving from an older Celtic root *ad-beron* 'to-bring'. Inver-, on the other hand, is from Gaelic

Inbhir [iñər] from an earlier *indo-bero 'in-bring'. (This word is actually cognate with English *infer* from Latin.)

Any reader familiar with Welsh place-names might recognise the element Aber- in names such as Aberystwyth and Abergavenny. This is because, as mentioned above, Pictish and Welsh are closely related languages. Other than the names listed in this book, Scottish examples include Aberchalder 'the inlet of the River Calder' and Aberdeen 'the inlet of the River Don'. One less obvious example is Applecross, this is on record as *Aporcrosan* in 673, and is at the foot of Abhainn Chrosain 'the Crossan River' [aviñ xrosin]. Over time, the name evolved into the form we know now, though it has nothing to do with apples or crosses.

Inver- names, although they are (almost) unique to Scotland, are much more numerous. Aside from those discussed in this book elsewhere, here are some examples. Inverugie from Gaelic Inbhir Ùigidh [iñər ooki] is the old name for Peterhead, at the foot of the river now called the Ugie. Inverness in Gaelic Inbhir Nis [iñər nish] at the foot of Abhainn Nis [awin nish] or the River Ness (from which Loch Ness flows). Inverroy or Inbhir Ruaidh [iñər rui] at the foot of the River Roy or Abhainn Ruaidh [aviñ rui].

This element is so popular that it was used in the New Zealand name Invercargill. Cargill here is not a river but the name of a Scotsman William Cargill who founded Otago in 1848. The settlement was named after him and Inver- was added to denote his Scottish ancestry.

Aberfeldy

Perthshire (*Abyrfeally beg* c.1300 meaning 'little Aberfeldy') [abərfeldi]

Aberfeldy is a name of Pictish origin, originally meaning 'the mouth of the (river) Peldy'. For Obar or Aber-, see p. 1. The original meaning of this river-name is not known for certain, but it could come from a root meaning 'distant' in the sense of 'deep' because the river has steep banks on either side. This burn flowing through Aberfeldy is now called the Moness Burn in English, and the area around it, the Moness Den.

The Gaelic form of the name is Obar Pheallaidh [opər fyauLi]. Gaelic was spoken in Aberfeldy up until the 1950s and the local Gaels had a tradition that the name Peallaidh was coined from the name of *uruisg* [oorishk], a sort of supernatural creature who lived in the upper reaches of Moness Den in a waterfall called in Gaelic Eas Pheallaidh 'Peldy's waterfall' [es fy<u>au</u>Li]. Other names in the area also refer to this supernatural creature, such as Caslorg Pheallaidh 'Peallaidh's track' [kas lorik fy<u>au</u>Li] and Ruighe Pheallaidh 'Peallaidh's slope' [rooyə fy<u>au</u>Li].

See also the Wonders of Scotland on p. 136.

Aberlogie

This is not a real place-name but is based on pre-existing elements combined in a novel way: Aber- (see p. 1) and -logie; the second of these is a fairly common place-name. As stated above, *aber-* is normally followed by a river-name, but Logie usually derives from a Gaelic name element. See **Glenlogie** for a discussion of that element.

Aberlour

Moray (*Abirlouer* in 1226)

The name Aberlour is Pictish in origin, from *aber* 'confluence' (see p. 1) followed by a river-name, thus the name means 'confluence of the river Lour'. The name is in Gaelic Obar Labhair [opər lawər – to rhyme with flower]. The river that flows through it is now however called in English 'the Burn of Aberlour'. *Labhair* in Gaelic means 'talkative', denoting the sound of the water as it flows along its course. A Lawer Burn flows down Ben Lawers near Loch Tay, giving its name to that mountain; this is also from this same root.

Abhainn Dearg

Lewis [<u>a</u>viñ j<u>e</u>rak]

Abhainn Dearg (or better, An Abhainn Dearg) is simply Gaelic for '(the) red river' from *abhainn* 'river' and *dearg* 'red'. There are two words for 'red' in Gaelic: *ruadh* [<u>ruə</u>gh] and *dearg* [j<u>e</u>rak]. *Ruadh* (which is cognate with English 'red' and 'ruddy') generally relates to a ruddy brown end of the colour spectrum and can also denote ginger hair. *Dearg*, on the other hand, is cognate with English 'dark' and represents the vibrant red seen in fire. The word can also be used as an intensifier, for instance, *dearg amadan* [jerak amatan] means 'a complete and utter fool'.

The lower part of the river by which the distillery sits is recorded on maps as Abhainn an Àth Dheirg 'the river of the red ford' [aviñ ən ah yerik]. An t-Àth Dearg 'red ford' [ən tah jerak] is nearby. It seems the distillery builders simplified the name. Upstream of the ford, the river is called Abhainn Caslabhat, which means 'the river of Caslabhat' where Caslabhat is the Gaelicised version of the earlier Norse name of the river. This contains an obscure first element followed by Old Norse *vatn* 'water'.

Ailsa Bay

Ailsa Bay is a new name but derives from the real-life name Ailsa Craig, a rock in the middle of the North Channel some way out from Girvan off the Ayrshire coast. This rock was previously known simply as Ailsa, the Craig was added by Robert Burns in one of his poems, and the new version stuck. Ailsa Craig is well remembered in Gaelic culture as *Allasa* or *Allasan*. This word Allasan is of unclear origin but may derive from Alt Shasann 'the cliff of the Saxons', referring to the Saxon settlements in Galloway prior to AD 800.

As far back as 1160, the Irish Book of Leinster describes it as *Aldasain i. carrac etir Gallgedelu 7 Cendtíri i n-a camar* (for *comar*) *immuigh*, 'Ailsa is a rock between Galloway and Kintyre, facing them out (in the sea)'. In more recent times a Gaelic insult was heard: *Is truagh gun robh thu eadar Allasan is* Àbhainn 'A pity but you were between Ailsa Craig and Sanda' used to express ill-wish upon somebody. (Àbhainn [aaviñ] is the Gaelic name for Sanda Island. This word is distinct from Gaelic *abhainn* 'river'.)

In Gaelic stories, Ailsa was sometimes referred to by different names such as Ealasaid a' Chuain 'Elizabeth of the ocean' [yeləsətch ə xu-in]; Creag Ealasaid 'Elizabeth's rock' [krek yelesitch] and in Irish Carraig Alasdair 'Alasdair's rock' [karik aləstər]. These names are likely reinterpretations of the name Allasan to make it understandable; there was no historical Elizabeth or Alasdair.

Ainsley Brae

This whisky is a blend, and there seems to be no such place as Ainsley Brae. *Ainslie's* is the name of another blended whisky made by James

Ainslie & Co, so it is possible the name was intended to be reminiscent of that blend. *Brae* is the Scots word for a 'slope' or 'hillside'.

Aird na Hogh

This appears to be a sort of Gaelic form of **Ardnahoe**.

Airigh nam Beist

Islay (*Ardnabest* in 1686)

This is now understood as Gaelic Àirigh nam Biast 'the shieling of the beasts'. The earlier form, however, suggests Àird nam Biast 'the height of the beasts'. *Biast* and *Bèist* are both loan words from Scots *beast*. Beist is how it appears on maps, but Biast is used by local Gaelic speakers.

Aldunie

Moray (*Auldeunye* in 1600) [oljuni]

The first syllable almost certainly comes from Gaelic *allt* 'burn, stream', the second element is less clear but may be from Gaelic *dìon* 'shelter' thus Allt Dìona 'shelter burn' [auLt jiiənə]. This burn is nowadays known as the Burn of Aldunie, upon which sits the settlement of Aldunie.

Alloa

Clackmannanshire (*Alloway* in 1359) [aloə]

This place-name is a combination of two Old Gaelic words: the first word is either *all* 'cliff' or *ail* 'rock', two similar words, both in form and meaning. The second word is *magh* 'plain', with the *m* changing by Gaelic grammar into a -v- sound. The name in Gaelic thus would have been something like Almhagh [aləvəgh]. North of Alloa is a place called Alva which is most likely of the same derivation, suggesting that a large area of the plain south of the Ochil Hills was once known as Almhagh, which now only survives in the names Alloa and Alva.

The name may also exist in the name of Alvie near Aviemore (see **Loch Alvie**).

Allt-á-Bhainne

Moray [auLt ə va̱ña̱]

This is a Gaelic name, which would be better spelled as Allt a' Bhainne; it means 'the burn of the milk'. This name is probably metaphorical, relating to the way the water froths 'like milk' as it flows. There are several burns with this name in the Highlands.

Anchor Bay

This whisky is handled by Lombard Whisky, a company situated in Ramsey on the Isle of Man. There is no place called Anchor Bay in Scotland or Man, but it may be a sort of description of Ramsey, the town in which Lombard is based, which is located by a bay on the coast.

AnCnoc

See **Knockdhu**.

Annandale

Dumfries and Galloway (*Estrahanent* in 1124)

Annandale comprises the name of the River Annan followed by Scots *dale* 'valley'. An earlier Gaelic version of the name spelled in 1124 is *Estrahanent* which suggests Srath Annan or, as it would be spelled nowadays, Strathannan. Strath is from Gaelic *srath* which means 'a broad valley' in Scotland. The name of the River Annan is ancient, and it possibly relates to the name of a goddess.

A Scots proverb about rivers in the south of Scotland runs thus:

> Annan, Tweed, and Clyde,
> Rise a' out o' ae hill-side
> Tweed ran, Annan wan,
> Clyde fell and brak its neck owre Corra Linn

In English:

> Annan, Tweed, and Clyde,
> Rise all out of a hill-side

> Tweed ran, Annan won,
> Clyde fell and broke its neck over Corra Linn

These three rivers all rise in the Lowther Hills, a mass of high ground in the south of Scotland. In the poem, the Annan, having the shortest course, won the race, while the Clyde was thought to have fallen and broke its neck at a large waterfall called Corra Linn on its course.

Arasgain
Renfrewshire

As explained on the back of the bottle, this is the commonly understood Gaelic form of Erskine, a place in Renfrewshire. The whisky is more specifically named after the Erskine Charity which cares for war veterans and is based in that town.

Arbikie
Angus (*Ardbekie* in 1573-4) [ar<u>biki</u>]

This is a name of Gaelic origin; the first element is Gaelic àird 'height' [aarshtch] as the early form suggests. The second element is unclear but might be related to Gaelic *beag* 'small' [bek]. See **Ardbeg** below.

Ardbeg
Islay (*Ardbeg* in c. 1591) [ard<u>beg</u>]

This place on Islay is called in Gaelic An Àird Bheag [ǝn aarshtch <u>vek</u>] meaning 'the small promontory'. Ardbeg is a common name, occurring several times in Scotland. See also p. 101.

Ardbeg had a special bottling called Ardbeggeddon, a name that is presumably a portmanteau of Ardbeg and Armageddon, the place mentioned in the Book of Revelations in the Bible where the final battle between good and evil is predicted to take place.

Ardenistle
Islay (*Ardinstill* in 1631) [ard<u>enistl</u>]

This place-name likely reflects Gaelic àird 'height' [aarshtch] followed by some sort of embedded Old Norse name ending with *dalr* 'valley', shortened in the English form to -stle. What the original Old Norse name was, however, we do not know.

TAUTOLOGIES

Much nonsense is said about tautological place-names. A tautology is something said the same way twice and which is therefore redundant, such as 'wet rain'. Concerning place-names, a tautological name would be something like 'Stone Rock', because all rocks are made of stones. A name such as Knock Hill in Fife, for instance, is sometimes thought to be tautological because Knock derives from Gaelic *cnoc* meaning – you guessed it – 'hill'. The common assertion is that it means 'Hill Hill'. This is not the case, however; the name means 'the hill of the place called Knock' where Knock comes from Gaelic *cnoc* 'hill'.

Ardgowan

Ayrshire (*Ardgowane* in 1499) [ardgauwən]

This is a name of Gaelic origin: Àird a' Ghobhainn 'the height of the smith' [aarshtch ə ghowiñ].

Ardlair

Aberdeenshire (*Ardlare* in 1402) [ardlər]

This is possibly from Àrd Làr or Àrd Làir '(the) high ground' [arsht laar]. There are other Ardlairs in Scotland that have this same derivation.

Ardmore

Islay and Aberdeenshire

There are two distilleries with this name. One was on Islay and has now been subsumed into the larger **Laphroaig** Distillery. The name Ardmore did not exist in this site before the distillery was built, and this name was possibly transferred from a 'real' Ardmore to the north east.

There is currently another Ardmore Distillery in Aberdeenshire. The site of the distillery is very far inland on fairly flat land, a landscape not suited for an *àird* or 'promontory'. It is not clear then why Ardmore was given as the name of this distillery, it having no apparent connection with the Ardmore on Islay.

Ardmore as a name comes from Gaelic An Àird Mhòr [ən aarshtch voor] meaning 'the big promontory'. See **Ardbeg**.

Ardnahoe

Islay (*Ardinhowe* in 1534) [ardnəh<u>o</u>]

This is in Gaelic Àird na h-Ò [aarshtch nə hoo] from àird 'height' and ò, thus 'the height of the place called ò or *hò*'. The place is referred to in documents as *Owo* or *How*, which is most likely a Gaelic adaption of a place-name from Old Norse *haugr* 'burial cairn'. There are indeed a number of mounds in the vicinity.

Ardnamurchan

Lochaber (*Artda Muirchol* in c. AD 700) [<u>ard</u>nə<u>murx</u>ən]

This, the most westerly point of mainland Britain, is from Gaelic Àird nam Murchan 'the promontory of the seals' [aarshtch nəm m<u>u</u>ruxən]. Although the name now denotes the whole peninsula, it originally denoted only the westernmost point where the lighthouse is now. The word *murchan* is from Gaelic *muir* 'sea' and *cù* 'dog', i.e. 'sea-dog'. This is an epithet for either a seal or an otter.

This name is, however, mentioned three times in *Vita Columbae* 'The Life of St Columba', a book written around AD 700 but pertaining to events in the sixth century. In this book, the promontory is referred to as *Artda Muirchol* (with variants). At this time, the name appears to have had a different final element, written here *-chol*. The meaning of this element is not clear, but it might be Gaelic *col* 'sin, wickedness', perhaps referring to acts of piracy or wrecking. Thus, the name may have originally meant 'the promontory of the (ship)-wrecking'.

Ardnave

Islay (*Ardnow* in 1507) [ard<u>neiv</u>]

This place is known to Islay Gaelic speakers as Àird Nèimh [aarshtch neiv] locally, using *àird* 'height' and *nèimh* 'holy' as if 'holy height'.

Earlier, however, the second element may have been some Norse place-name that was later Gaelicised as Nèimh.

Ardtalla

Islay (*Ardtalloch* in 1541) [ard ta̱La]

This is a Gaelic name: Àird Talla 'the height of Talla' [aarshtch tawLa]. *Talla* is likely a Norse place-name, possibly from *Háland* 'high land', changed by folk-etymology into *talla* which is Gaelic for 'hall'.

Arran

Argyll (*Arand* in the tenth century)

This is the name of a well-known island in the southern Hebrides. In Gaelic, it is called Arainn [ariñ], but, like many names of the larger islands in the Hebrides, the original meaning is unknown, despite several valid suggestions. A beautiful Gaelic poem of the tenth century refers to Arran as *Arand na n-aighedh n-imdha* 'Arran of the many deer'.

The water source for this distillery is known as Loch na Davie on maps, from Gaelic Loch na Dèabhaidh 'the loch of drying or evaporating' [lox nə je̱ivi], from its habit of drying up in warm weather.

Auchavan

Glen Isla (*Achvane* in 1747–55) [oxə̱van]

The name of this small settlement is of Gaelic origin being something like Achadh Bhan, from *achadh* 'field, farm' followed by a second element. What *Bhan* represents is not entirely clear. The name may represent Gaelic An Achadh Bhàn 'the white field', but in this name *achadh* 'field' is feminine, whereas it is always masculine elsewhere. Alternatively, it may represent the name in a different syntactic position. This is to say if you were to say 'in Auchavan' in Gaelic, this may have been said as 'anns an Achadh Bhàn', and then this was adopted as the main form.

Auchenhame

There is no such place as this in Scotland; this name is most likely a portmanteau. The first element is Auchen-, a common prefix in Scottish place-names (see p. 11). The second part, -hame, is the

Scots word for 'home'. This name does not have a meaning, rather it is more likely supposed to simply evoke Scottishness.

Auchenlone

Dumfries and Galloway [oxənloon]

The settlement Auchenlone in Dumfries and Galloway no longer exists, although Auchenlone Burn still survives on maps. It is a southern Gaelic place-name, most likely reflecting what would be in modern Gaelic Achadh an Lòin 'the farm of the marsh'.

Auchentoshan

Dumbartonshire (*Achintaissan* in 1654) [oxəntoshən]

This name is said to be from Achadh an t-Oisein 'the field of the corner' or even 'the corner of the field'. This, however, is not very good Gaelic; the form would be *Achadh an Oisein [axadh ən oshin]. A place nearby Auchentoshan is Oceanfield which looks to be a part translation of the name, whereby Gaelic *achadh* is translated as 'field', and the -*oshen* part adopted and reanalysed as English *ocean*. Ocean Field was well-known as a site containing Roman artefacts. Whilst the name Auchentoshan is certainly Gaelic and the first word is *achadh* 'field', the identity of the second element -toshan is unclear.

The water source for this distillery is Loch Katrine, for this name see **Glen Catrine**.

AUCH- /ACH- / AUCHTER-

The majority of Scottish names beginning with Auch- or Ach- are from the Gaelic element *achadh* [axəgh]. This term originally denoted simply a 'field' but evolved into meaning a 'farm' and then a 'settlement'. Not all place-names beginning with these syllables derive from *achadh*, however. For example, Acharracle is from Gaelic Àth Tharracail [ah charrachkil] from *àth* 'ford' and a personal name Tarracal a form of Torquil, thus 'Torquil's ford'. Likewise, names beginning with Auchter- often derive from a completely different Gaelic word: *uachdar* meaning 'upland' or 'upper part of a region' [uəxkər]. See **Auchtertyre**.

Aucherachan

See **Auchorachan**.

Auchinblae

Aberdeenshire (*Auchynblay* in 1506) [oxənblei]

Whilst the whisky is spelled Auchinblae, on maps the place-name is written Auchenblae. Although we cannot now be sure of the original form, since Gaelic has not been spoken in this area for so long, it probably derives from a name which would be spelled in the old form of the language as *achad ind blá*, from Old Gaelic *achad* 'field', *ind* 'of the' and *blá* which can mean 'a boundary marker' or an area demarcated thus, such as 'a level field or green'. Alas, more than this we cannot know.

Auchindoun

Moray (*Auchindoun* in 1491) [oxəndun]

This name survives on maps now as Auchindoun Castle; it is from Gaelic Achadh an Dùin 'the farm of the fort' [ax ən dun], where the fort or *dùn* no doubt denotes the site of the castle here.

Auchnagie

Perthshire (*Auchnagie* in 1835) [oxnəgee]

This is a name of Gaelic origin: Achadh na Gaoith 'the farm or field of the wind' or 'the windy farm or field' [axnə gw-i]. Although the distillery is now closed, the settlement still exists, written on maps as Achnaguie.

Auchorachan

Moray (*Achorrachan* in c. 1591) [oxorəxən]

This name is on record in Gaelic as Achadh Chorrachain [axə xorəxən]. *Achadh* means 'farm or field' whilst *corrachan* can have several meanings: 'a stilt', 'a jackdaw', 'herons' or 'storks'. We do not know which of the meanings, if any, was originally intended.

Auchroisk

Moray (*Auchquhroskie* in 1554) [oxrosk]

Auchroisk is from Gaelic Achadh a' Chrosgaidh 'field of the crossing' [axə xroski]. This name is sometimes said to mean 'ford on the red stream'. This appears to be a misunderstanding on a number of points: there is another Auchroisk in Cromdale, but this is in Gaelic Àth (a') Chroisg meaning 'the ford of the cross'. The derivation of 'red stream' for -roisk is unclear but may be thought to come from the Gaelic word *ruadh* 'red'.

A map of c. 1591 shows two settlements marking *Achroisk oc:* and *Achroisk ic:*. These two abbreviations stand for Gaelic *uachdarach* 'upper' and *iochdarach* 'lower' respectively, thus meaning Upper and Lower Auchroisk.

Auchtermuchty

Fife (*Uchtermukethin*' in 1205–11) [oxtər mʌxti]

This name is often mentioned as being a quintessentially Scottish name, sounding 'funny' to some ears, probably because of the repetition of the -cht- cluster which contains sounds that do not appear in most English dialects. The Auchter- part of the name comes from Gaelic *uachdar*, 'upland'. The second element is likely Gaelic *mucadaidh*, whose precise meaning is not clear, although it may mean 'pig burn', the Gaelic for 'pig' being *muc*. Thus, the name most likely means 'the upland of the Muchty Burn'.

The Auchtertyre

[oxtər tair]

There are several places called Auchtertyre in Scotland. For the one in Perthshire at least we know this was in Gaelic Uachdar Thìre 'upper part of land' [uəxkər hiirə]. See p. 11.

The Auld Brig

Ayrshire

This whisky is part of the Robert Burns Collection, which all have names concerned with that man's life and works. In a poem called 'The Brigs of Ayr', he imagines an argument or 'flyting' between the New Brig (i.e. the new bridge) and the Auld Brig (i.e. the old bridge) in Ayr. *Brig* is the Scots word for 'bridge'.

Auld Reekie

Edinburgh (*Auld Reekie* in 1724)

This is an affectionate name for Edinburgh meaning 'old smokey', coined from the smoke coming from the densely packed tenements.

Aultmore

Moray (*pastura in Auldmoir* in 1571) [olt<u>moor</u>]

This name is an excellent example of how place-names can be deceptive. On the face of it, Aultmore would seem to simply represent Gaelic An t-Allt Mòr 'the big burn'. This, or something similar, is what you will read in various books, supposed to denote either the River Isla or the Burn of Aultmore. The water source for the distillery itself is the Auchinderran Burn to the west of this area.

The truth is not so clear-cut as it would seem, however. Aultmore actually denotes a high ridge of moorland rather than a watercourse. In 1742, it was described as a 'hill called Old-More, where one may travel five miles all upon fine heather; under which lies moss ground'.

The name might be taken to be a Scots version of Old Moor, but a spelling in c. 1591 refers to it as *Moore of Ald* as if Ald or Ault were a place-name already. Therefore, the name appears to be Scots, meaning 'the moor of the place called Ald'. (*Moor* in Scots can also mean a hilly area.) The origin of the word Ault or Ald is unclear, but perhaps it comes from an Old Gaelic word *alt* usually meaning a 'cliff', 'rock', or perhaps most relevant here 'upland'

Badachro

Ross and Cromarty (*Baddichro* in 1566) [<u>bat</u>ə<u>xroo</u>]

This is from Gaelic Bad a' Chròtha 'the copse of the (cattle) pen' [bat ə xroha].

Bad na h-Achlaise

Ross and Cromarty [baatnə haxlishə]

This is Gaelic for 'the copse of the armpit' or 'oxter' as it is called in Scotland. *Achlais* in place-names denotes an armpit-shaped concavity in the ground. See **Badachro** above.

Balblair

Ross and Cromarty [balblair]

This is a common name which comes from Gaelic Baile a' Bhlàir 'the farm or town of the field or plain' [balə vlaar]. Sometimes *blàr* can mean a battlefield; it is also referred to in nearby Carriblair which is from Gaelic Blàr a' Charaidh 'the field of the grave' [blar ə xari]. In local folklore, a sculptured stone here is said to mark the grave of a Danish prince called Carius.

The water source for this distillery is said to be 'The Allt Dearg', which is Gaelic for 'red burn'. There is, however, no watercourse with this name in the area, although it is possible that Craigroy Burn is intended. There is another Allt Dearg a short distance away but this is in another watershed entirely and flows into Strathrory.

Balcarron

There is no such place as this in Scotland, but it is a product of **Dailuaine** Distillery which is situated near a place called Carron. This name is from Gaelic Caran, possibly meaning 'twists' in relation to the turning of the River Spey here. Balcarron appears to relate to this place-name, but with Bal- added on, as if from Gaelic *baile* 'farm, town'. Thus the Bal- is equivalent to the 'whisky glen' (see p. 68).

Balgownie

Aberdeenshire (*Palgoueny* in 1256; pons de *Polgowny* in 1480) [balgauni]

The whisky called Balgownie is named after a bridge over the River Don in Aberdeenshire called 'the Brig O' Balgownie'. A text from 1654 says of it: 'the bridge of Done called the bridge of Balgonie'. Place-names beginning with Bal- usually related to Gaelic *baile* 'farm', but in this case, the early forms and context show that the word was Gaelic *poll* 'pool'. The second element may reflect either *gobhainn* 'blacksmith' [go-iñ] or *gamhainn* 'stirk, young bull' [gau-iñ].

BAILE / BAL-

Many Scottish place-names begin with Bal- or Bally-; these generally come from Gaelic *baile*, a word originally meaning 'farm' but which later came to denote 'village' or 'town'. *Baile* was a very fashionable Gaelic place-name element and it appears as far south as Lothian and as far north as Caithness.

Ballaglass

Isle of Man (*Ballaglass* in 1643) [baləglas]

Although a Scotch, the place Ballaglass is located on the Isle of Man, a small island between Scotland and Ireland that has its own version of Gaelic called Manx. This place-name is what would be written in Scottish Gaelic as Baile Glas 'green farm' (see above).

Ballantruan

See **Old Ballantruan**.

Ballechin

Perthshire (*Balechan* in 1654) [baləxin]

The name of this Perthshire estate is from Gaelic Baile Eachain 'Hector's farm'. *Eachan* [exan] is a Gaelic personal name, often translated into English as Hector, although the names have no etymological connection.

Local tradition states that Eachan or Hector was the son of James II, King of Scots (1430–60). This is not quite true, although James II did have an illegitimate son called John Stewart of Stix who had a child called Patrick Stewart who was 1st Laird of Ballechin. There is no historical mention, however, of anyone called Eachan or Hector.

Ballindalloch

Moray (*Balnadalloch* in c. 1591) [baləndalox]

Ballindalloch is Gaelic Baile na Dalach 'the farm of the river-side haugh' [balə nə dalox]. *Dalach* is a reflex of *dail*, see p. 48.

Ballochmyle

Ayrshire (*Bellachmill* in c. 1636–52) [balox mail]

This is Gaelic, from Bealach (na) Maoile 'gap of (the) bald hill'. Gaelic has not been spoken in Ayrshire for several centuries, so the exact form of the name is difficult to reconstruct.

Balmenach

Moray (*Balmeanach* in 1747–55) [balmenox]

This is from Gaelic: Am Baile Meadhanach 'the middle farm' [əm balə me-anox]. Nearby there is a farm called Ballachule which is from Gaelic Baile Chùil 'back farm' [balə xul], therefore it seems likely there was once another farm on the other side of Balmenach with a name meaning 'front farm', thus making Balmenach 'the middle farm'.

Balmoral

Aberdeenshire (*Bouchmorale* in 1451) [balmorəl]

Balmoral was originally Gaelic Both Mhorail 'the hut or church of Moral' [boh voril] although the latest generation of Gaelic speakers called it Baile Mhorail [balə voril]. Here, *both* 'hut or church' and *baile* 'town, farm' have become muddled. (See p. 16.) To add to the confusion, Easter Balmoral is Baile a' Mhorair Shìos 'upper town of the lord' [balə voril hiiəs], whilst the land above Balmoral is known as Bràigh Mhorail [brai voril] 'the upland of Moral'.

The element *moral* is from Pictish, related to Gaelic *mòr* 'big' and meaning a 'great, clear space', possibly denoting a large clearing in a forest. It appears in other names such as Polmorral or Poll Mhorail 'the pool of Moral' on the River Dee near Banchory.

Balnellan

Moray [bal<u>ne</u>lən]

This is Gaelic for Baile an Eilein 'the farm or town of the island' [bal ən yelin]. For *baile*, see p. 16. Balnellan is indeed a small Strathspey settlement by the River Avon by a small unnamed island in the river.

Balvenie

Moray (*dominio de Balvany* in 1579) [bal<u>ve</u>ni]

Although this name is clearly Gaelic, the exact meaning is not clear. It is mentioned in a Gaelic poem as Baile Mhanaidh [balə vani] in the line 'S *tha thu d'mhòir-fhear Baile-mhanaidh* 'and you are the lord of Balvenie'.

For *baile*, see p. 16. The second element could be *manadh* [manəgh], meaning 'apparition or omen', the whole thing thus meaning 'the farm of the apparition' although this is far from certain.

The water source for this distillery is said to be from 'Robbie Dhu (or Dubh) Spring'. Robbie Dubh would mean 'dark (haired) Robert'. There is, however, no corroborating evidence for this name and no evidence at all for it before a string of newspaper advertisements in the 1970s.

Banff

Aberdeenshire (*Banb* c. 1150)

Banff is a well-known region and town of Scotland, called Banbh, [banu] in Gaelic, which is an old word meaning 'suckling pig'. This is either (like Atholl) meant to denote a poetic term for Ireland or was an original name for the River Deveron on which the town of Banff sits. The names of larger animals are quite common in the names of larger rivers.

The Banks O'Doon

Ayrshire

This whisky commemorates the Robert Burns' poem of the same name. The Doon is a river in Ayrshire, Burns' home county. The river-name is Celtic in origin, likely from a root *dēouana possibly simply meaning 'goddess'. O' is Scots for 'of' so in modern English we would say 'the banks of the (river) Doon'.

(Old) Bannockburn
Stirlingshire (*Bannauc* in 1200)

This has a complicated history. The name of the current settlement known now as Bannockburn takes its name from the watercourse that runs through it: Bannock Burn. This first appears in a Latin text written around AD 1200; from the context this most likely refers to the hills to the west of Bannockburn. It is mentioned in medieval Welsh literature as the boundary between the Britons of the Old North and the Picts. The name in British most likely meant 'abounding in summits or spurs'.

After the battle that took place here in 1314, the place was mentioned many times in Gaelic writing, usually referred to as *Allt a' Bhonnaich* 'the burn of the bannock'; a *bannock* being a type of flat bread. This is a translation of the newer Scots form of the name, which has no historical authenticity. There is a Scots rhyme which refers to the battle, which also propagates this folk-etymology:

> The burn of Breid
> Sall rin fu' reid

In English:

> The Burn of Bread
> Shall run full red.

The reference to red here is the blood of the battle, whilst the name Bannockburn has been referred to as 'the Burn of Bread'.

Banoch Brae

There is no such place as this in Scotland. Banoch does not appear anywhere in Scotland and was most likely constructed to sound Scottish. *Brae* is Scots for a 'hillside'.

Barra

Western Isles (*Baray* in 1549)

Whilst the second element in this name is derived from Norse øy 'island', the first element is not certain. Norse *berr*, 'naked', 'bare' or *barr*, 'rough'. Several Hebridean island names seem to have uncertain derivations, suggesting they may derive from earlier pre-Celtic roots which are unknown to us.

There is, however, a church on Barra called Cille Bharra meaning 'Saint Barr's Church' [kîlə vara]. It is therefore possible that the island was named in Norse after this saint, who was also known as Findbarr and Finnan.

Barrogill

Caithness (*Baregil* in 1606)

This place on the northern tip of mainland Scotland is most likely Norse in origin, but the specific elements remain unclear. The -gill is most likely Norse *gil* 'gully', but the identity and original meaning of *barro* is not clear.

Barstruie

There is no such place as this in Scotland. There is a place in Easter Ross called Struie, which is in Gaelic An t-Sruidh 'the stream place' [ən tru-i]. Given that Barstruie is a 'Ross-shire Malt', it is therefore likely that its name was coined from this Struie, with Bar- added. In place-names, Bar- is normally from Gaelic *bàrr* 'hill', and is very common in Scottish place-names.

Battlehill

Aberdeenshire

There is a tradition that this hill takes its name from the Battle of Slioch, a skirmish fought nearby in 1307 between John Comyn, Earl of Buchan, and Edward Bruce during the Scottish Wars of Independence. There is little historical evidence to support this, however.

Bealach Ruadh

Islay

Bealach Ruadh is Gaelic for 'red pass' [byaləx ruə] and the road out of Port Askaig runs through it. A nearby settlement is called Ballochroy which is an anglicised form of the name.

Beinaigen

See **Ben Aigen**.

Beinn a' Cheo

[beiñ ə coo]

Beinn a' Cheo (better, Beinn a' Cheò) is Gaelic for 'the mountain of the mist'. Although there is no place marked on maps in Scotland with this name, it does appear several times in poetry. It is unclear if it is just a poetic description of any particular mountain, or an old lost name for an existing one.

Beinn Dubh

Beinn Dubh means 'black mountain' in Gaelic, and whilst there are several mountains with this name in Scotland, it is unlikely the name refers to any specific one. Instead, *dubh* meaning 'black' most likely reflects the colour of the whisky itself, which is very dark.

Beldorney

Aberdeenshire (*Baldorny* in 1491) [beldorni]

This name appears to be Gaelic Am Baile Dòrnach 'the pebbly farm' [əm balə durnox] or Baile Dòrnaidh 'farm of the pebbly place' [balə durni]. A famous Gaelic poetess, Sìleas na Ceapaich, was associated with this place, but unfortunately, she never wrote the name down in Gaelic in any of her poems, so we cannot be sure of the exact Gaelic form of the name.

Bellfield

Edinburgh (*Bellsfield* in 1824)

Bellfield refers to an area in Portobello, Edinburgh, which appears locally as Bellfield Street and Lane. The 1824 form suggests the name Bellfield was coined after an individual called Bell, but his or her identity is unknown.

Benachie

Aberdeenshire (*Benechkey* in 1355–57) [benəhee]

This is the name of a well-known mountain in Aberdeenshire. In Gaelic, it is often referred to as Beinn a Chì which has been interpreted as 'the hill that you see' although it actually means 'a hill that sees'. Although this belief is quite well established, in origin it has a different form. *Beinn* is for Gaelic 'mountain'; this is not in doubt. It is not clear, however, what the *chì* element may have originally been; it may have related to the name of an ancient Pictish Kingdom called Cè. Perhaps this mountain was considered to be at the centre of it.

Ben Aigen

Moray (*Bin Eygen* in c. 1591) [ben eigin]

This name is coined from the name of a hill near the River Spey which is written on modern maps as Ben Aigan. It comes from Gaelic Beinn Èiginn 'mountain of difficulty' [biñ eikiñ], so coined from one of its sides, which is very steep.

Ben Aros

There is no such place as this in Scotland, but there are various places called Aros, which is a name of Norse origin, from *Áross* 'river mouth'.

Ben Bracken

No such place as this exists in Scotland. It seems to be a fabricated name from Ben as if from Gaelic *beinn* 'mountain' and Scots *bracken*.

Ben Cally

There is a small possibility this name is coined from Benachally, a mountain in Clunie Forest in East Perthshire. This is from Gaelic Beinn Challaidh [biñ xauLi] where *beinn* is 'mountain'; the second word is, however, obscure in meaning. Alternatively, there are several watercourses around Scotland with the name Cally, but none near Port Ellen on Islay or Leith in Edinburgh, where this whisky was respectively made and bottled.

Benderloch

Lochaber (*Beandir Loch* in c.1640) [bendərlox]

This name was at some point in the past Beinn Eadar Dà Loch 'the mountain between two lochs', relating to the mountainous region in Argyll between Loch Creran to the north and Ardmucknish Bay and Loch Etive to the south. The English form of the name is simply a shortened version of this old Gaelic form. The modern Gaelic, however, is Meadarloch [metərlox].

The exact reason for this change is not clear, but the initial B- in the name may have become nasalised by influence with the word *an* 'in', earlier Gaelic *in*. Thus, Early Gaelic *i mBeinn Eter Dhá Loch* 'in Benderloch', where -mb- was pronounced simply as -m-. The -nn- in the word beinn may have become lost by dissimilation between the new initial nasal -m- and the -nn. That is, there were too many nasal sounds in the word.

Beneagles

This name originates in the name Gleneagles (*Glennegas* in 1482), which has been subject to several interpretations – in both Gaelic and Scots – influencing the form of the name over time. The first element Gaelic *gleann* 'glen' [glauN] is not in doubt; the second or specific element, however, may have originally been from Gaelic *eagas* 'notch-place' [ekəs] a derivative of *eag* 'notch' [ek]. This was not readily understandable in Gaelic, however, and it seems to have been interpreted later as Gaelic *èagas* 'bard or learned man' [ekəs].

It is not until the seventeenth century that forms with -l- appear, such as *Gleneglis* in 1630. The name appears to have been reanalysed yet again as Gaelic Gleann na h-Eaglais 'the glen of the church' [glauN nə heklish], possibly by non-local Gaelic speakers who used this glen for droving cattle. Finally, within a Scots context, the Gaelic word *eaglais* was reinterpreted as if it were the Scots English word *eagles*, leaving us with the modern form, Gleneagles.

The whisky was originally called Peter Thomson's Whisky, but its name was changed to Beneagles, specifically in reference to the Gleneagles Hotel. As with other names, the Ben- here is entirely fabricated. The connection with eagles is strengthened by the depiction of that bird on the bottle.

Ben Èideann

This non-existent name is based on the Gaelic name for Edinburgh which is Dùn Èideann [dun eijeN]. *Dùn* means 'fort' or 'hill which could have a fort on it', *Èideann* as a word no longer exists in Gaelic, and it may come from a Brittonic word meaning 'ox'. In this name, however, Dùn has been swapped for Ben, see p. 68.

Ben Gullion

Kintyre, Argyll (*Ben Goilen* in 1747–55) [ben gulyun]

This refers to a hill overlooking Campbeltown, which is written as Beinn Ghuilean on modern maps. This is a Gaelic name, from something like Beinn Gualann 'shoulder hill'. Two shoulders, formed by a deep notch, are plain to see.

Ben Ledi

Stirlingshire (*Ben Ladhia* in 1747–55) [ben ledi]

This is the name of a mountain, in Gaelic Beinn Lididh [biñ litchi], of unknown meaning. There is a Gaelic tradition that the name is actually Beinn le Dia 'the mountain with God' (as suggested by the early form above), but this is not supported either by the pronunciation or the context.

Benloyal

Sutherland (*Bin Loyall* in c. 1591)

The name of this mountain is from Gaelic Beinn Laghail [biñ laghil].

Beinn is of course Gaelic for mountain. *Laghail* or *Laghal* is itself from Old Norse, either *Lagavöllr* 'law field' or *Lagafjall* 'law fell', presumably denoting a place where Viking settlers met to dispense justice. Ben Hee and Ben Hope are nearby mountains, and there is a Gaelic proverb about the three:

> Thuirt Beinn Shìth ri Beinn Hòb, 'Nach e tha mòr Beinn Laghail? Nam faighinn às am paiseanadh mòr, chuirinn sgòrr dhe Beinn Laghail'.

> Ben Hee said to Ben Hope, 'Isn't Ben Loyal big? If I could get free in a great passion, I would knock a peak off Ben Loyal'.

Ben MacDhui

Aberdeenshire

This is the second tallest mountain in Scotland and is from Gaelic Beinn MacDuibh, 'the mountain of the MacDuffs'. The Duff family owned part of Ben Macdui for centuries and this hill was named after them.

Ben Morven

There is no such place as Ben Morven in Scotland, but there are several mountains called simply Morven, the two most notable being the ones in Caithness and Aberdeenshire. They both come from Gaelic A' Mhòr-Bheinn 'the big mountain' [ə voor veiñ]. Given that *beinn* 'mountain' already appears in the name Morven, we would not expect it to appear again as Ben. This name is entirely distinct from Morvern.

See also **Glen Morven**.

Ben Nevis

Lochaber (*Bin Neuesh* in c. 1591)

This is from Gaelic Beinn Nibheis [biñ nivish]. *Beinn* of course means 'mountain'. Nevis or Nibheis was originally the name of the river which flows past the mountain, called in Gaelic Abhainn

Nibheis (*Auon Neuesh* in c. 1591) 'river Nevis'. This is an old river-name possibly linked with an Old Celtic root *nebh-* 'cloud, water, moistness'.

Ben Nevis, being the tallest mountain in Britain, appears in some Gaelic proverbs, normally concerning anti-climaxes. One goes:

> Thuit Beinn Nibheis, is gun d'aithnich mi sin air a turachail an-raoir.

> Ben Nevis has fallen, and I knew that would happen by its swaying last night.

This is a cynical remark made when a small accident occurs.

The water source for this distillery is Allt a' Mhuilinn 'the mill burn' [auLt ə vuliñ].

Benriach

[ben<u>riox</u>]

This is not a genuine place-name. Near to the distillery is a place called Riach; in all likelihood Ben- has been added on to this name. Riach most likely comes from a Gaelic adjective *riabhach* meaning 'speckled or brindled' [riox or riəvox]. Apparently, the place was once covered with louse-wort which in Gaelic is called *lus riabhach* 'brindled plant' [lus riəvox], or even simply *riabhach*. It seems then that the name may be a reference to that.

Benrinnes

Moray (*Bel Rinnes M* in 1654)

This is Gaelic name originally, probably from Beinn Ruanais [biñ ru̠anish]. *Beinn* means 'mountain', whilst *Ruadhanais* perhaps means 'red place', thus 'mountain of the red place'. The water source of this distillery is from two burns which merge near the summit of Ben Rinnes. The first is Rowantree Burn and the second Scurran Burn. Scurran is from Gaelic Sgurran 'a small pointed hill' [skuRan]. There are several of these in the area.

Benromach

This distillery takes its water from the Burn of Mosset which rises in Romach Hill some distance to the south. Ben is an anglicised form of *beinn* meaning 'mountain or hill'. I can find no evidence that Romach Hill was ever called Ben Romach or *Beinn Ròmach [biñ <u>room</u>ox]; whilst it is possible the name was Gaelicised for effect, it is also possible that the owners of the distillery knew the hill as Beinn Ròmach in Gaelic, and used the name accordingly. Gaelic *ròmach* means 'furry' or 'shaggy', so the name could have meant 'shaggy mountain' from the vegetation on it.

Ben Roland

This is an invented name from Ben- as if from Gaelic *beinn* 'mountain' and the personal name Roland. This whisky was sold by Glen Stuart, which is another invented name containing a personal name.

Ben Royal

This is not a place-name. Ben Royal was a brand created for the Silver Jubilee of Queen Elizabeth II in 1977. Doubtless, the 'Ben' part was to reflect the fact that it was a Scotch, with the 'Royal' part to commemorate the Jubilee. It may also be a pun on the name of Ben Loyal (See **Benloyal**).

Benveg

There is no such place as this in Scotland. If there were, it would most likely be from Gaelic Beinn Bheag 'small mountain' [biñ vek].

Ben Wyvis

Ross and Cromarty (*Ben Ouish* in 1747–55) [ben weevs]

This mountain name is from Gaelic Beinn Uais [biñ uish]. *Beinn*, of course, means 'mountain' and *uais* is from the same root as seen in the Gaelic word *uasal* 'high, noble', thus the name might mean something like 'mountain of nobility'. *Uais* is not a word commonly understood, however, so sometimes the name was written Beinn Fhuathais, with the same pronunciation, as if meaning 'spectre mountain'.

Blackadder

The name of this bottling company is not, strictly speaking, coined from a place-name. The name of the company was coined from John Blackadder, a Scottish covenanter who died in 1686. His surname was coined from a settlement called Blackadder in Berwickshire, which was itself named from its situation on the banks of Blackadder Water. The name of this watercourse is called Black to differentiate it from the Whiteadder Water into which it flows. Adder as a river-name is likely an ancient Celtic river-name, of uncertain meaning.

Black Burn

Inverness-shire

This is a bottling of the **Speyside** Distillery, and near their site on the banks of the River Tromie is a burn called Fèith Dhubh [fei ghu] which means 'black burn' in Gaelic. Therefore, it seems likely that the name was taken from this burn and translated into English. See p. 159.

Black Cuillin

Skye

The Cuillins or Coolins are a famous mountain range on Skye; they are divided into the Black and Red Cuillin, and this whisky is coined from the former. The name the Cuillins is from Gaelic An Cuiltheann which is itself perhaps from Old Norse, but it is not clear what Norse words would fit the derivation. Several Gaelic derivations have been offered, mainly relating to mythology, but none of these are suitable.

Bladnoch

Dumfries and Galloway (*Bladnoch* in 1477) [bladnox]

Bladnoch was originally the name of a river that gave its name to the settlement of Bladnoch. Many names of larger rivers are very old, and this name likely goes back to a pre-Gaelic British language. The exact meaning is unclear but may well relate to a root *blọd* which can mean 'flour' or possibly a separate root coincidentally meaning 'flower'.

Blainrow

There is no such place as Blainrow, although there is a Blainroe in County Wicklow in Ireland. In Irish, this is *An Bhléan Ruadh* probably meaning 'the red hollow'.

Blair Athol

Perthshire (*Blar in Atholia* in 1451)

This Perthshire place-name is in Gaelic Blàr Athall 'the clearing of the place called Atholl' [blaar awoL]. The name Atholl itself most likely comes from an early Gaelic Ath Fhodla perhaps means 'second Fodla', where Fodla may mean 'portion, share'. Alternatively Fodla may be a commemorative name for Ireland. Atholl was an early Gaelic kingdom which evolved from a previous Pictish-speaking territory. Blair Atholl was the centre of this, and it is possible that the original name was a simple Pictish name Blar, with Atholl added on to differentiate it from Blairgowrie, where Gowrie is the name of another nearby territory.

Blair or Blair Atholl is mentioned in a Gaelic poem, as Strath Atholl (see p. 148).

Gabhaibh an rathad as fheàrr,
Srath Athall, is bhur casan cho geàrr,
Is ma theirgeas an latha mu Bhlàir,
Is ro mhath an t-àite a ghabhail tàimh.

Take the best road,
Strath Atholl, your feet being so short,
and if the day ends about Blair,
It is a very good place to take a rest.

The water source for this distillery is a burn now called Kinnaird Burn, but was formerly called Allt Dobhair Shuas 'upper burn of Dour'. See the entry for the nearby **Edradour** which contains the same element.

Blairfindy

Moray (*Blairfindy* in c. 1591) [blair fin̲di]

This name is likely of Gaelic origin, though the exact form is not clear.

The first element is probably *blàr* 'field' and the second part -findy most likely relates to Gaelic *fionn* 'white'.

YE OLDE GHAELIC H

We have already seen how the addition of Ben or Glen to a name makes it seem more 'Scottish'. Another similar device is the insertion of an h after an initial consonant. For instance, in Edinburgh there is a bar called Ghillie Dhu and another called An Cait Dhu. They look sort of Gaelic, don't they? This is because modern Gaelic orthography (a posh word for spelling) uses an h after a consonant to change the sound. Thus, b is pronounced as in English, but bh is pronounced as an English w or v. Similarly, Gaelic mh is generally pronounced as a v; ph as f (as in English) and so on. This is such a departure from English orthography that it looks distinctively Gaelic and is used as such as a marker in order to make something look Gaelic and therefore more 'authentic' or 'ancient'. Some names of whiskies employ the same device: Knockdhu, Blairmhor, Lochdhu, Dallas Dhu, Corriemhor, Cardhu, Tamdhu and Glen Mhor. None of these when spelled as such conform to Gaelic spelling or syntax. All of the spelling changes centre around representations of two Gaelic word *mòr* 'large' and *dubh* 'black'.

Blairmhor

[blair<u>vor</u>]

This is not a place-name as such, being a blend of Speyside malts. It is a combination of the element Blair from Gaelic *blàr* 'field' and -mhor from Gaelic *mòr* 'large' as if the name means 'big field', although the -h- should not be there (see above).

Borders

The Borders in Scotland simply denotes the southernmost region in Scotland, forming the border with England.

Bowmore

Islay [bo<u>moor</u>]

The Gaelic form of the name is Bodha Mòr 'big sunken rock' [boə moor]; The word *bodha* can relate to a bend (as seen in the bay here), or a sunken rock; *mòr* means 'large'. Normally, however, one would expect a definite article in Gaelic names of this type, as in Am Bogh Mòr 'the big bend'. The lack of one might suggest the name was originally a Viking or Norse name from Old Norse *boði* 'reef' (whence Gaelic *bodha*). This name was then taken over into Gaelic as Bodha and Mòr was added later.

Brackla

Nairnshire (*Bracklay* in 1802)

Brackla is from Gaelic A' Bhraclaich [ə vraxklic]. This is, most likely, a variant of *broclach* 'badger warren' [broxklax]. The water source for this distiller comes from the nearby Cawdor Burn. Cawdor as a name is identical in origin with the various rivers in Scotland called Calder. (See Glen Calder.)

Braemoray / Braymoray

Moray (*Bramurrey* in c. 1591)

Braemoray is from Gaelic Bràigh Mhoireibh 'the upland of Moray' [brei v<u>u</u>riv]. This is from Gaelic *bràigh* 'upland' and Moireibh or in English Moray, a district of Scotland. See Glen Moray for more details. With Scotland being so mountainous, many district names have an 'upland' or mountainous area. Braemar is in Gaelic Bràigh Mhàrr 'the upland of the district of Mar' [brei vaar].

Braes of Glenlivet

Moray

Brae is a Scots word for a slope or hillside, and when used with a place-name means 'the upper part'. See **Glenlivet**.

Braeval

Moray [breival]

This is from Gaelic Bràigh a' Bhaile 'the upland of the farm' [brei valə] the -val bit of the name is an oblique form of Gaelic *bhaile* 'farm' seen in the names beginning with Bal- (see p. 16). The *baile* or farm in question is surely Belnoe nearby, which is probably from Gaelic Am Baile Nuadh 'the new farm' [əm balə noə]. Braeval occurs several times throughout the Highlands.

Bridge of Allan

Stirlingshire (*Bridge of Allan* in 1747–55)

This name means 'the bridge over the River Allan', where Allan represents a pre-Gaelic Celtic river-name element which appears elsewhere in the British Isles, such as in the names Inverallan, Alne Water, Alness and Allander. In modern Gaelic, it is called Drochaid Ailein, which means on the face of it 'Allan's Bridge' [droxitch alin]; nearby is Strathallan or Srath Ailein likewise meaning 'Allan's strath'.

Bridge of Avon

Moray (River Avon is *Ain R:* in c. 1591)

This name is as it sounds, the bridge over the River Avon. There are many rivers in the British Isles called the Avon, and this one is a tributary of the River Spey. Received wisdom says that the name Avon goes back to an Old Celtic *Abonā*. This word is cognate with Gaelic *abhainn* 'river', but this is not to say this river-name Avon comes directly from *abhainn*, rather they have a common origin.

Another derivation, however, goes back to an Old Celtic form *ate-vinda* 'most bright one'. This derivation fits the modern Gaelic form better, which is Athfhinn [a-iñ]. A much later Gaelic story casts Athfhinn as the wife of Fionn, an old Gaelic hero. The story goes that Athfhinn fell in, and Fionn names the river after her, saying:

Uisge bhàin nan clachan sleamhainn!
'S an deach mo bhean a bhàthadh;
'S e Athfhinn a bheir mi air an abhainn.

Fair water of the slippery stones!
Wherein my wife was drowned,
Athfhinn (Avon) I will name the river.

See also **Inveravon**.

Brodgar

Orkney (*Brogar* in 1832)

Brodgar in Orkney is famous for the astounding standing stones known as the Ring of Brodgar. This is a name of Norse origin, supposed to be from *Brúargarðr* 'bridge farm'. Brodgar sits on the Ness of Brodgar, a tongue of land that almost connects with Stenness. Nowadays the two bits of land are connected by a bridge of unknown date. The name of the settlement nearest Brodgar is called Bridgend.

Brodick Bay

Arran (*Brodick Bay* in 1769)

Brodick is a name of Norse origin, from *Breiðavík* 'broad bay'. The local Gaels on Arran had two names for Brodick and its bay at various times. The earlier term was Breadhaig [brei-ik] which is the Norse version of Brodick, coming from the same Norse root. Mostly however, the bay and settlement were called Tràigh a' Chaisteil 'the shore of the castle' [trai ə xashtchil], after the imposing Brodick Castle situated here.

Brora

Sutherland (*Strabroray* for Strathbrora in 1499)

This name is from Gaelic Brùra which itself is from Norse *Brúará* meaning 'bridge river'. The site of the original bridge across the river here is not known. See **Brodgar** above.

Bruichladdich

Islay [bruic latic]

This is from Gaelic Bruthach a' Chladaich 'the slope of the shore' [bru-ox ə xlatic]. A range of these whiskies is called Bruich Laddie. This actually reflects the local Islay Gaelic pronunciation of *chladaich* [xlatic] as *chladaidh* [xlati].

Bunnahabhain

Islay [bun nə haviñ]

This is a Gaelic name: Bun na h-Abhainn 'the foot of the water' [bun nə haviñ]. *Bun* in Gaelic means the foot or base of something, whilst *abhainn* means 'river'. The river in question is called Abhainn Araig 'the river of Araig'. This name Araig is of Norse origin, perhaps from Árvík 'river bay', which is similar in meaning to Bun na h-Abhainn.

Since whisky needs flowing water for the distillation process, it is no surprise many of the place-names contain water words.

See also **Abhainn Dearg**.

Burn O' Bennie

Kincardineshire (*Burn of Benie* and *Burn of Benavie* in 1636–52)

This name appears on maps as Burn of Bennie, but locally *of* is pronounced as *o'*. This name is applied both to a burn or watercourse as well as a small settlement. *Burn* is the Scots word for a stream, but the meaning of Bennie is less clear. The early form above of *Burn of Benavie* might suggest that the same root as found in Banavie or Banbhaidh [banəvi] in Fort William. See Banff for more information on that word.

Bùrn Taobh

This is very bad Gaelic for 'burnside'. Although there was a Burnside Distillery in Campbeltown, this whisky is a blend of Speyside malts, so it seems unlikely this is an attempt at a translation. A better translation of Burnside would be Taobh an Uillt [twv ən eeltch] or even Taigh an Uillt 'the house by the burn' [tai ən eeltch].

Cabrach

Moray (*Cabrach* in 1654) [kabrox]

This Cabrach is in Moray but there are several places in Scotland with this name. This particular one is called in Gaelic A' Chabraich 'the place of tree-stumps' [ə xap̱ric], from Gaelic *cabar* 'pole, cabre'. In English, it is also often called The Cabrach.

Caermory

There is no such place as Caermory. This whisky was made at **Tobermory**. Perhaps the name is a portmanteau using the second part of that name combined with another name beginning with Caer-. Alternatively, Caer- could have simply been swapped with Tober-.

Cairn Guish

Moray [kairn gush]

This hill name is from Gaelic Càrn a' Ghiuthais 'the hill of firs' [karn a yu-ish]. *Càrn* can mean both a 'cairn' in the sense of a heap of stones and also a cairn-shaped hill. *Giuthas* is the Gaelic word for 'fir'. See also **Drumguish**.

Cairnleigh

There is no such place as this in Scotland, although there is a Cairnleigh Drive in Houston, Texas, which is located amongst other street names coined from Scottish places. Place-names with Cairn- in them generally come from either Scots *cairn* or Gaelic *càrn* both meaning 'a heap of stones'. Possibly, the name relates to Cairnlea or Cairnleith.

Cairnluish

There is no such place as Cairnluish in Scotland. Place-names with Cairn- in them generally come from either Scots *cairn* or Gaelic *càrn* both meaning 'a heap of stones', but -luish does not appear in Scottish place-names. This whisky is an alternative name for Tamnavulin, and to the south of that settlement, there is a **Cairn Guish** on the slopes of Ben Rinnes to the north. Possibly Cairnluish is some sort of adaption of this name.

Calchou

The label on the bottle depicts Kelso Abbey and states the contents were bottled by Roxburgh Holdings Ltd which was based in Kelso. Thus, it is perhaps no surprise that the name *Calchou* is an early spelling of the place now known as Kelso. Although this name may have earlier Celtic origins, it appears that Calchou and Kelso come ostensibly from Old English *calc hōh*, 'limestone or chalk height'.

Cambus

Stirlingshire (*Cambus* in 1584)

Cambus is the name of a settlement outside Stirling, near a bend in the River Forth. Cambus is undoubtedly from Gaelic *camas* which means either 'a bend in a watercourse' or 'a curved bay'. In this instance, it has the first meaning. The River Forth is very winding here, and other nearby places such as Cambuskenneth and Cambusbarron contain the same element.

Cameronbridge / Cameron Brig

Fife

This Bridge in Fife is named after a nearby settlement called Cameron and is not named after the common Scottish surname. Cameron (*Cambrune* in c. 1250) is likely a Pictish place-name in origin comprising perhaps *cam* 'crooked' and *bren* 'hill'. For the distillery, English *bridge* was added later to denote a separate nearby place. A single grain whisky made by the distillery is called Cameron Brig, here *brig* is the Scots word for 'bridge'.

Campbeltown Loch

Kintyre, Argyll

Campbeltown is known in Gaelic as Ceann Locha 'loch end' [kyauN loxə] or more fully as Ceann Loch Chille Chiarain 'lochend of Kilkerran' [kyauN lox xìlə xi-ərin]. Kilkerran (now a part of modern Campbeltown) is from Gaelic Cille Chiarain meaning 'the church of Ciaran'. See Kilkerran for a discussion of that saint. The English name Campbeltown is relatively modern, having been coined in 1667 by Archibald Campbell, Earl of Argyll. A charter records the change of name: 'therefor erecting the said town of

Lochead [i.e. Ceann Locha] into a free burgh of barony, to be called the burgh of Campbeltoun'. Campbeltown Loch itself was known in Gaelic either as Loch Chille Chiarain, ie. Loch Kilkerran, [lox xi̬lə xi-ərin] or, strangely enough, as Loch Ceann Locha 'the loch of Kinloch' or 'the loch of the end of the loch' [lox kin loxa].
See also **Kinloch** and **Kilkerran**.

A GAELIC POEM ABOUT CAMPBELTOWN LOCH

In 1855 or 1856 the Gaelic bard William Livingstone or Uilleam MacDhunlèibhe wrote a poem about a fictional battle called Blàr Shunadail, 'the battle of Sunadale' in Kintyre. In this poem, he mentions Campbeltown Loch and gives several Gaelic place-names, which he may well have heard during a visit. The relevant passage reads:

Le gaoth nan siùil, 's ràimh gan sparradh
Gu dian an iar ag iarraidh rathaid
Gu loch fasgach Chille Chiarain,

Miann nam bàrd 's na chunnaic riamh e!
Ràinig na seòid Cleit a' Chaolais,
Eadar Eilean dà Bhàrr is Creag nam Faoileann,
Òb fasgach, is gun tonn air cladach.

With wind in their sails, and oars propelling them
Eagerly westwards, looking for a way
To sheltered Loch Kilkerran

The desire of the bards and those who have ever seen it!
The menfolk reached Cleit a' Chaolais,
Between Island Davaar and Creag nam Faoileann
A sheltered bay, without waves at the shore.

Here Campbeltown Loch is called 'Loch Kilkerran'. The location of Cleit a' Chaolais and Creag nam Faoileann are alas unknown.

The Canongate
Edinburgh (*Canovngat de Edynburgh* in 1366)

The Canongate in Edinburgh is a name of Scots origin. *Canon* means a sort of religious cleric, and here relates to the Augustinian canons of Holyrood, nearby. *Gate* in earlier English and Scots did not mean what it means today, but rather a 'way' or 'street'.

Caol Ila
Islay [kwl iilə]

This name means 'the straits of Islay' in Gaelic. *Caol* in Gaelic means 'slender' or 'a narrow stretch of water'. Ila is a slight misspelling of Ìle, the Gaelic form of Islay [iilə]. The -s- in Isla is inorganic or 'false', it was inserted on analogy with words like *isle* and *island*. In Gaelic 'a person from Islay' is an Ìleach which is also the name of a whisky as well as the name of the local newspaper.

There are in fact three places with the name Caol Ila. The original place is the stretch of water between Islay and Jura. The second is the name of the settlement beside this strait. The third is the peat bog where the peat is dug to make the whisky. The first and third of these are called Caol Ìle in Gaelic. The second, however, is called Ruadhphort in Gaelic, meaning 'red port'. It was originally called Freeport by the mining company.

Caol Ila's water source is Loch nam Ban 'the loch of the women' [lox nəm ban], a fairly common name.

Caperdonich
Moray [caperdonic]

Caperdonich Distillery was originally called Glen Grant 2 when it was built as a backup to Glen Grant in 1898. It closed soon after and was reopened in 1965. In the intervening time, a law had been passed prohibiting two distilleries having the same name, so it was renamed Caperdonich, allegedly from 'a small on-site burn that supplied its process water'. The source was said to be variously a 'secret well' or 'secret burn'. On maps, however, Tobar Dòmhnaich [topər dõnic] is marked quite clearly; this is Gaelic for 'the Lord's Well'. Caperdonich is an anglicisation of this name, possibly using the first half of the Biblical place-name Capernaum, where Jesus lived for some time.

The Ordnance Survey says of this well in the 1860s: 'An ordinary spring formerly a resort of pleasure parties it is now cased in and the waters are conveyed to Glengrant house for domestic use. It is traditionally recorded to have possessed rare medicinal qualities and is regarded as a holy well'.

Cardhu

Moray [kar<u>duu</u>]

Cardhu is a variant spelling of Cardow, a nearby settlement, and this spelling was used until 1981. This name comes from Gaelic An Càrr Dubh 'the black bog' [ən kaar duu]. See p. 30 for the spelling of -dhu.

Carlton

This is the name of a blended whisky and does not seem to relate to a place-name. There is no place in Scotland with this name, although it is quite common in England.

Càrn Mòr

This is a bottling company, and as such this is not a distillery site. The company should be given full marks for retaining the Gaelic *sracs* or accent marks on the vowels in this name, which denote that the vowels are long. Càrn Mòr means 'large cairn or cairn-shaped hill'. There are dozens of these in the Highlands, and it is not clear which one, if any, is referred to here

Carraig Dubh

Islay [karik du]

This should be Carraig Dhubh [karik ghu] according to Gaelic syntax. There is a number of places with this name in the Highlands, and they mean 'black sea rock'. The most famous and most likely one meant here is Carraig Dhubh, situated in Loch Indaal off Islay. A small settlement on the coast near Carraig Dhubh is called Blackrock which is simply an English translation.

Carraig Dhubh is mentioned in an Islay Gaelic tongue twister which mentions various nearby places as well:

Cailin dubh à Eorabus,
Cailin donn an Carrabus,
Cailin chridheil Uisge an t-Suidhe,
Luisrichean na Carraige Duibhe,
'S Pioraitean Charnàinne

A black-haired girl from Eorabus
A brown-haired girl in Carrabus
A cheerful girl of Uiskentuie
Leprechauns of Carraig Dhubh
And pirates of Carnain

Carsebridge

Clackmannanshire (*Carsebridge* in 1783)

This place-name is from Scots *carse* 'a low fertile land by a river' and Scots *bridge*. It may be that the Brothie Burn was previously called the Carse Burn, named after an area of Carse to the south, and thus the name meant 'Bridge over the Carse Burn'. The distillery was built up around the bridge.

Caskieben

Aberdeenshire (*Caskyben* in 1261)

The name Caskieben was originally applied to Keithhall Castle, but it was moved to a place in Dyce, Aberdeenshire. It possibly comes from Gaelic An Gasg Bàn 'the white tail (of land)' [ən gask baan].

Clachaig

Lochaber [klaxik]

This is a place in Glencoe now known as Clachaig Inn, after which this whisky is presumably named. Clachaig [klaxik] is a diminutive of Gaelic *clach* 'stone' meaning 'little stone' or rather 'place of little stones'. This place is mentioned in a poem: *Mi gam fhogradh à Clachaig* 'Me, banished from Clachaig'.

Cluny

The longer name for this blend is MacPherson's Cluny; many clan chiefs of the MacPhersons are called 'MacPherson of Cluny' so it seems sensible that the name related to this. The Cluny in this title then relates to the clan stronghold Cluny Castle in Strathspey. Nonetheless, Cluny or Clunie is a relatively common name in Scotland, deriving from Gaelic Cluanaidh meaning 'meadow place' [klu̱əni]. Today in Gaelic if someone is retired one would say he or she is *air cluain* literally meaning 'on the meadow' or 'out to pasture'.

Clutha

The name of Clutha is taken from Macpherson's Ossianic Poetry which used *Clutha* as the Gaelic name of the River Clyde. Macpherson likely invented this form for his poetry, however, since the name of the Clyde in Gaelic is *Cluaidh*, and he was well-known for fabricating things. See Strathclyde for a discussion of the name of the Clyde.

Clynelish

Sutherland (*Clynlish* in 1747–55) [klain lish]

This name has two parts to it. The first part Clyne is in Gaelic Clìn [kliin]; this is the local Sutherland dialect pronunciation of the Gaelic word *claon* 'slope' [klwn]. This place, Clyne or Clìn, is divided into several places, one of which is Clynelish. -lish comes from Gaelic *lis* from *lios* meaning a 'garden or enclosure'. Thus, the name means 'Clyne of (the) garden'. Also nearby is Kintradwell, in Gaelic Clìn Trolla 'the Clyne of St Trolla or Triduana' [kliin tro̱Lə] and Clynemilton or Clìn a' Mhuilinn 'Clyne of the mill' [kliin ə vu̱liñ].

The name of the stream used by the distillery is An t-Alltan Donn 'the brown stream' [ən ta̱Ltan dou̱N].

Cnoc Lart

This whisky is made in 'a secret distillery on Islay', and whilst there is no such place as Cnoc Lart on Islay or indeed anywhere else in Scotland, there is a Cnoc Iart beside the Caol Ila Distillery. Could it be that when choosing the name for this whisky, Cnoc Iart was misread on a map as Cnoc Lart? Gaelic *cnoc* [kroxk] means 'hill'; the meaning of *iart* is not known, although *iar* means west and the hill sits somewhat north-west of Port Askaig.

Cockburns

[ko<u>ub</u>urnz]

This whisky name does not derive directly from a place-name but is named from a company called Cockburn & Co. It was established in 1796 as a Leith wine and spirit merchant by brothers John and Robert Cockburn. The surname Cockburn itself is named from a place in the Borders, near Melrose (*kokeburn* in 1285) which comes from Scots *cock* 'waterfowl' and burn '*stream*' (see p. 159) thus 'waterfowl's stream'.

Coleburn

Moray (*Colburn* in 1747–55)

This is a Scots name, from *burn* 'stream, brook' (see p. 159). The first element is unclear but could relate to Scots *cole* 'coal' or *cole* 'cool, cold'. It could even relate to *cock* 'rooster' or 'waterfowl'. One source claims the element relates to coal mining, but there is no history of industrial coal mining in this area.

Convalmore

Moray

This name appears several times throughout Scotland and probably are all Gaelic Conmheall 'combination of lumps' [kon-vyauL]. Alternatively, it is from an early Pictish formation related to the Gaelic form. The ending -more looks to be from Gaelic *mòr* 'big'.

There is no place at this site called Convalmore but nearby on the other side of the Dullan Water are two hills called Meikle Conval (*Conwall* in 1747–55) and Little Conval. *Meikle* is Scots for 'big'. It might be that Convalmore is a sort of Gaelicisation of Meikle Conval, where Scots *meikle* is translated into Gaelic *mòr*.

Corgarff

Aberdeenshire (foresta de *Corgarf* in 1507)

The first syllable of this word represents Gaelic *coire* 'corrie', a word originally meaning 'a kettle' but used in place-names to denote a dip in a mountainside. The second element is not clear, but it is perhaps Gaelic *garadh* 'den or cave', (perhaps meaning an animal's den) thus Coire a' Gharaidh 'the corrie of the den' [korə a ghari] The -ff in the English form looks as if it were from Gaelic *garbh* [garav] 'rough' but the Gaelic pronunciation does not support this.

Corriemhor

Corriemhor is not the name of a distillery but a type of whisky. It therefore does not seem to relate to a real place. If it did, it would be from Gaelic *coire* 'corrie, or hollow in a mountain' and *mòr* 'big'. For the h in mhor, see the Ghaelic h (see p. 30).

Corryhabbie

Moray (*Coryhabbie* in 1832) [korihabi]

This name is locally pronounced simply as Corhabbie, reflecting the local pronunciation of Gaelic *coire* 'corrie' [koirə] as coi' [koir]. The name is from Gaelic: Coire Chabaidh 'the corrie of notching or notch-places' [koir xapi].

Corryvreckan

Argyll [kori-vrekan]

The Gulf of Corryvreckan is a small strait at the north end of Jura which contains a dangerous whirlpool. In Gaelic, this gulf is called Coire Bhreacain meaning 'Breacan's kettle' [koirə vraxkin], the idea being that the sea here is boiling and frothing. The identity of Breacan is unclear, folklore has attributed the name to various things, but as it stands, it means 'speckled one'. In Gaelic, the whirlpool itself was called A' Chailleach 'the hag' [ə xailyox], who was thought to be a supernatural creature responsible for the sinking of boats.

Corshelloch

Moray [korshelox]

This is from Gaelic An Coire Seileach 'the willow corrie' [ən koirə shelox].

Coylumbridge

Inverness-shire [koiləm brij]

In Gaelic, it is called Drochaid na Cuinghleim [droxitch nə kõiləm] meaning the same thing as the English form, although locally this place is often simply called Coylum. This is from Gaelic A' Chuingleum 'the gorge leap' [ə xõiləm], referring to a rocky narrow place at the bridge here over the River Druie, across which it is possible to leap, or at least was perceived that someone could leap. There are several Coylums in the Highlands of Scotland, and many of them have stories associated with them about someone who had jumped across during a chase, unfortunately in this case we do not have any associated tradition.

Cragganmore

Moray [kragan mor]

This distillery was named after Craggan More, a hill situated to the south of the distillery described by the Ordnance Survey as 'A high bold hill, the north side of which is for the most part covered with fir woods'.

This name is from Gaelic An Creagan Mòr 'the big rocky place' [ən krekan moor]. *Creagan* can mean 'a rocky place' or 'a little crag'. There is another Craggan to the south of this place, and it is possible the word *mòr* 'large' was used to differentiate it from this other Craggan.

CRAIG, CRAG AND CREAG

Craig in Scottish place-names, all things being equal, is from Scots *crag* or *craig* or Gaelic *creag*, all meaning the same as English *crag* or rock, in the sense of a rocky outcrop when inland, and a sea-rock when by the coast.

Craigardle

There is no such place as Craigardle in Scotland. This whisky is rebranded Blair Atholl whisky; near that place is Strathardle and the River Ardle, which this name presumably denotes. Ardle is from Gaelic Àrdail 'high place' [arshtəl]. To this existing name, Craig appears to have been prefixed (see p. 44).

Craig Athol

Craig Athol is another fabricated name. The name Athol (as spelled in this name) derives from the area known as Atholl; see Blair Atholl for a discussion of that name. Craig has been artificially added to the real name (see p. 44).

Craigduff

This was made at Glen Keith Distillery in Keith, so most likely this relates to the **Duff of Dufftown** twenty miles away. Craig is added in a similar way to Glen- and Ben-, see p. 68.

Craigellachie

Moray (*Kraig-Elachy* in c. 1591) [kraig eُlaxi]

There are two places with this name in Strathspey, giving rise to the proverb: *Eadar an dà Chreag Eallachaidh* 'Between the two Craigellachies'. This is supposed to denote the whole of Strath Spey, although one is by Charleston of Aberlour and the other by Aviemore, which hardly denotes the whole of the strath. Craigellachie was also the war cry of the clan Grant.

The name is Gaelic of course, from *creag* 'crag' with an existing place-name Eallachaidh which, most likely, means 'rock place'.

Craiglodge

This Whisky is in a range with Croftengea and Glen Douglas. There are several places with this name in Scotland and this bottling could be named after one of these, or it could be completely invented. On the face of it, the name looks to be Scots *craig* 'crag' and English *lodge*.

Craignure

Isle of Mull [kraig<u>nyoor</u>]

This place-name is from Gaelic Creag an Iubhair 'crag of the yew tree' [krek ən yuwər].

Creag Isle

This is the name of a blend and is not the name of a real place. *Creag* is Gaelic for 'crag' and it appears to be this word with 'isle' added on.

Croftengea

Dumbartonshire [kroftənge-ə]

This is the name of a croft whose present location is now in Alexandria, Dunbartonshire. Its derivation is not clear but the first part of it represents Gaelic *croit* 'croft' followed by the definite article. The -gea portion is possibly *geadh* 'goose'. This would give Croit a' Gheòidh 'the croft of the goose' [krotch ə yi-oo-i].

Crois Chill Daltain

Islay [krosh ciïl daltin]

This is Gaelic for the Kildalton Cross, which is a monolithic Celtic Cross in Kildalton parish church on Islay. Cill Daltain means 'church of Daltan' [kiïl daltin]. *Daltan* means a foster son, denoting here St John the Apostle.

Cromdale

Inverness-shire (*Krombell* in c. 1591)

Cromdale is in Gaelic Crombail [kroumbil], but the English form is likely closer to the original form of *crom-dhail* 'crooked river-side haugh'. See p. 48.

Culdrain

Aberdeenshire (*Coldrane* in 1511)

This is an early name of Gaelic origin, possibly from *còmhdhail* 'assembly, court site' plus *draigheann* 'blackthorn' thus perhaps meaning 'assembly place or small court distinguished by a thorn-tree'. Coldrain in Kinross has the same derivation.

Cùl na Creagan

There is no such place in Scotland with this name, as far as the author is aware. It may, however, be a place on Sleat in Skye that is not on published maps. Broadly speaking, it means in Gaelic 'the back of the crags'.

Cullicudden

Ross and Cromarty (*Culicuden* in 1227) [kʌlikʌdən]

This is of Gaelic origin, from Cùil a' Chudainn 'the nook of the cuddy' [kuul ə xutiñ]. A cuddy is a sort of fish. Nearby is Drumcudden which is Druim a' Chudainn 'the ridge of the cuddy' [drim ə xutiñ].

(Royal) Culross

Fife (*Cuilendros* in 800–900) [kuros]

This name is Gaelic Cuileann Ros 'holly point' [kuuləN ros]. The early form comes from an Old Irish text which reads: *Cuilendros hi Sraith Hirend hi Comgellaib itir sliab n-Ochel acus muirn-Guidan* 'Culross in Strathearn in Comgellaibh between the Ochils and the Forth'.

Culzean Castle

South Ayrshire (*Culzeane* in 1501) [kəlain]

Culzean is a difficult name to parse, but it may be from Gaelic Cùil Sìthein, 'nook of fairy hill' [kuul shii-in]. *Cùil* is the word for a hollow, nook or corner, whilst *Sìthean* [shii-an] is the word for a 'fairy hill', that is, a small hill in which the Gaels believed fairies lived. A short distance further inland from Culzean is a mound called Shean Hill, and this could be the Sìthean referred to in the name of Culzean.

Cumbrae Castle

Argyll (*Kumreyjar* in 1263) [kʌmbrei]

Cumbrae Castle is situated on the island called in English Little Cumbrae, next to Great Cumbrae, both near the Isle of Bute. These two islands are called jointly in Gaelic Cumara. This name is of Norse origin, from *Kumreyjar* 'land occupied by the Cymry or Cumbrians', although the name may have been reinterpreted over time. A Gaelic proverb about the islands states:

Chan ann am Bòd uile tha an t-olc, ach an Cumara Bheag tha làmh ris. 'It is not in Bute alone that the mischief is, but in Little Cumbrae beside it'.

DAIL, DAL, DOL AND DALR

Gaelic *dail* denotes a 'riverside meadow', and thus appears in many distillery names, since these must be near a river or stream; it is often anglicised as Dal- in place-names. The Picts had an earlier word *dol* of the same meaning; this appears in some names such as Dull or Dallas mentioned below. It may be that some Gaelic names with *dail* earlier came from Pictish *dol*.

A Germanic cognate of these words exist, giving English and Scots *dale* and *dell*. This word also occurs in names of Norse origin as *dalr* in names ending in -dale, such as Spinningdale or Armadale. In these cases, the words mean simply 'valley' rather than a riverside meadow.

Daftmill

Fife (*Dafmylne* in 1500)

This name means 'the mill on the Daft Burn'. The Daft Burn or Daft Water is now called Ballantagar Burn and the Rankeilour Burn but is on record as *Daft Burne* in 1654. The river-name Daft most likely is Gaelic in origin, from *damh* 'ox' or 'stag'. Many river-names derive from names of animals, often denoting the way they flow. Thus, the name may mean 'river which roars like an ox'. The name has later been reinterpreted as Scots *daft* 'daft, stupid'.

Dailuaine

Moray [dal <u>uu</u>-añe]

There is no evidence for this name before the distillery was built. Other names containing Gaelic *dail* are spelled Del- in the area, such as Deldonald. If this is a genuine name, it would be from (An) Dail Uaine meaning '(the) green river-side meadow' [ən dal <u>uu</u>-añe]. This distillery is fed by the Burn of Carron. See **Balcarron**.

Dalaruan

Kintyre, Argyll (*Dalaruan* in 1832) [d<u>a</u>lar<u>uu</u>ən]

The Gaelic form of this name was recorded about a century ago as *Dail a rùdhain* which perhaps reflects Gaelic Dail (an) Ruadhain 'meadow of the red thing or place' [dalə <u>ruu</u>ən]. Exactly what the red thing relates to is not clear, however. On the other hand, there was an Irish saint called Ruadhán, so perhaps he is commemorated here. See also Lochruan which contains the same element.

Dalchully

Inverness-shire (*Dalchulie* in 1747–55) [dal<u>xu</u>li]

This is from Gaelic Dail a' Chuilidh [dal ə <u>xu</u>li] 'the river-side meadow of the hollow'. The river in question is the Spey.

Dallas Dhu

Moray [dales duu]

The first word in this name, Dallas, is a settlement near the distillery. This name is from Gaelic Dalais [dalish] (older *Dolais*), perhaps of Gaelic origin or from an older Pictish place-name meaning 'meadow place'. In 1226 it is on record as *Dolays Mychel* meaning the 'Dallas of (St) Michael'.

The second word Dhu looks as if it comes from Gaelic *dubh* 'black' [duu], but that part is fabricated, most likely to give the name a Gaelic flavour. The distillery was built by Glasgow blenders, Wright & Greig Ltd, who were also the proprietors of Roderick Dhu, a whisky brand that was popular in the nineteenth century, which was coined from Walter Scott's character from *The Lady of the Lake.* Therefore, it is possible Dhu was added to enforce a connection with their other whisky brand. See p. 30. Some books claim the name means 'black water valley', presumably as if Gaelic *Dail Ghlais Dubh, or 'field by the dark waterfall' as if *Dail Eas Dubh, but these derivations do not make sense grammatically, nor do they reflect the linguistic history.

The Texan city of Dallas is named after George Mifflin Dallas, the eleventh vice-president of the United States (1845–49) who was of Scottish descent; thus, his surname was presumably coined from the Scottish town of Dallas.

Dalmore
Ross and Cromarty

The original place called Dal More applied to a triangle of land to the north-east of the River Alness stretching between the distillery of Dalmore and the sea. It comes from Gaelic An Dail Mhòr 'the big riverside meadow' [ən dal voor].

Dalmunach
Moray

Dalmunach is a Gaelic place-name in origin, the first element is *dail* 'water-side meadow' (see p. 48), but the second element is unclear. It could relate to an old Gaelic word *mungach* 'shaggy, overgrown'. Alternatively, the surname Munn, Gaelic Munna, could be present here, as in Dail (a') Mhunnach, 'the haugh of the Munns' [dal ə vuNox]. Both these suggestions are speculative, however.

Dalrymple Bridge
Ayrshire (*Dalrympil* in 1371)

Dalrymple is most likely a name of Gaelic origin, but the exact form is unclear. The first syllable is likely *dail* 'river-side meadow' but the -rymple part does not suggest anything in Gaelic. Locally the name is pronounced *Darumple*. Dalrymple Bridge is a real bridge within the town.

Dalvegan

There is no such place-name as this in Skye, rather it appears to be based on the Skye place-name Dunvegan, with Dal- swapped for Dun-. See **Dun Bheagan** for discussion of Dunvegan.

Dalwhinnie

Inverness-shire (*Dalwhinnie* in 1747–55)

Dalwhinnie is a Gaelic name Dail Chuinnidh [dal xuñi]. The first element is *dail* 'water-side meadow'. The second element is less clear but is probably a word meaning 'champion' from Old Irish *cuingid*, *cuinnid*.

Dalwhinnie was a famous coaching station in days gone by and the following Gaelic verse shows how much progress could be made in one day:

> Bracaist ann am Baile a' Chloichridh
> Lòn ann an Dail na Ceàrdaich
> Dìnneir ann an Dail Chuinnidh
> 'S a' bhanais ann an Ràt

> Breakfast in Pitlochry
> Lunch in Dalnacardoch
> Dinner in Dalwhinnie
> And the wedding in Logierait.

The name of the burn which serves the distillery is Allt an t-Sluic, a Gaelic name meaning 'the burn of the pit' [auLt ənt looick].

Dark Cove

This was made by **Ardbeg** Distillery and there is no such place as Dark Cove, rather the word 'dark' denotes the fact that this was matured in dark sherry casks. The box proclaims it to be 'the darkest Ardbeg ever'.

Davaar

Kintyre, Argyll (*Insulam Daabhara* in 1393) [da<u>var</u>]

Davaar refers to Island Davaar, a famous tidal island just off the coast of Kintyre, just beyond Campbeltown Loch. The name is nowadays referred to in Gaelic as Eilean Dà Bhàrr 'the island of two summits', despite this not being a particularly appropriate name. In 1436, however, it was referred to as *insula de Sanctbarre*, which is Latin for 'the island of Saint Barre'. This tells us the name was thus originally Eilean do Bharr 'the island of saint Barre'. *Do* here means 'your' or 'thy' and was used honorifically to denote a saint. Barre was an Irish saint associated with Cork in 830; he was also known as Finnan.

Deanston

Stirlingshire (*Denstoun* in 1585)

Deanston is situated in the Highlands on the River Teith. It is a name of Scots origin, meaning most probably 'the farm of the dean', likely relating to the dean of the nearby Dunblane Cathedral. It is not related to the name of Doune. In 1657 it was referred to as *Sauchintoune alias Deanstoun*. This variant name is from Scots meaning 'willow farm', from Scots *sauchen* 'willow' and *toun* 'farm'. It is probably not a coincidence that there is a farm called Sauchens nearby.

Deeside

Aberdeenshire

Deeside relates to the area around the River Dee in Aberdeenshire. This name is first on record as *Deoua* as far back as AD 150, by the twentieth century it was known in Gaelic as Dè, as seen in the phrase: *Tha Dè mòr an-diugh* 'the Dee is full today'.

There was a riddle about the Dee: *A' chraobh a leag mi an-diugh, thuit i an-dè* 'the tree I felled today, fell yesterday'. This was a pun on the word *an-dè* 'yesterday' which would mean 'in the Dee' if spelled *an Dè*. Thus, the sentence could also mean 'the tree I felled today fell into the Dee'.

The Deveron

Moray (*aquam de Douern* 'the water of the Deveron' in 1273)

In all likelihood, the name of this river represents Gaelic Dubh-Èireann, meaning 'black Ireland'. This is presumably a commemorative name, also seen in the name **Atholl**. A few miles away is the river Findhorn, and this most likely comes from a Gaelic Fionn-Èireann 'white Ireland'. Here, 'black' and 'white' are used to differentiate one from the other; this is a phenomenon which occurs from time to time with river-names. The river-name Èireann or Èire appears elsewhere in Scotland, usually appearing on maps as Earn.

Dhoon Glen

Isle of Man (*the Dooin* in 1729)

This name relates to a place which is not in Scotland but on the Isle of Man. It relates to a place called the Dhoon, which most likely comes from Manx Yn Dowin which would be written in standard Scottish Gaelic as An Domhain meaning 'the deep or steep place' [ən do̱win]. The glen does indeed have steep sides running to the sea. *Glen* is simply Manx English added to it.

Dhunomhainn

(*Dunon* in 1264–66)

This whisky commemorates the 1994 Dunoon Mòd. A *mòd* is a celebration – in competition form – of Gaelic arts, involving singing, dancing and storytelling. The name Dhunomhainn is a sort of version of the Gaelic form of Dunoon though it would better be spelled Dùn Omhainn [duun owiñ]. Many variant forms of this name are found. *Dùn* is Gaelic for 'fort' but the meaning of the second element is unclear.

Dornoch

Sutherland (*Durnach* in 1214) [do̱rnox]

This is a Gaelic name, Dòrnach meaning 'place of pebbles' [doornox], presumably in relation to the beach here. In modern Gaelic, *dòrn* means a 'fist'. A well-known place-name proverb dubs this place Dòrnach na gorta 'Dornoch of the famine'. This epithet no longer holds true.

Drumadoon Point

Arran (Druimadoun or Carban Point in 1814)
[drʌməduun point]

The name Drumadoon is from Gaelic Druim an Dùin 'the ridge of the fort' [drim a duun]. Nearby stands the eponymous fort, called The Doon in English and An Dùn [n duun] in English. Drumadoon Point specifically has had several names, including Rubha an Dùin 'the promontory of the fort' [rooa ən duun], as well as Carban Point, which is not readily explainable.

Drumblade

Aberdeenshire (*Drumblathe* in 1403) [drʌmblet]

This is a name of Gaelic origin. The first element is *druim* 'ridge' but the second element is obscure, it may be the same element as seen in **Bladnoch**, a Pictish root meaning 'flour'.

Drumbowie

[drʌmbaui]

There are several places in Scotland called Drumbowie, and they come from Gaelic An Druim Buidhe 'the yellow ridge' [ən drim buyə].

Drumguish

Inverness-shire [drʌm guush]

This is a Gaelic name, Druim a' Ghiuthais 'the ridge of the pinewood' [drim a yoo-ish]. It is very near Kingussie which is Ceann a' Ghiùthsaich 'the end of the pinewood' [kyauN ə yuusic]. It seems likely therefore that pines were once common in the area.

Drumlassie

Aberdeenshire [drʌmlauzi] (*Drumlaussy* in 1540)

The first element in this name is certainly *druim* 'ridge', but the identity of the second element is unclear. Locally, the second half of the name is pronounced -lawsie, and this element is also seen in nearby Birselawsie or Birselasie, whose first element may be Gaelic *preas* 'woods' [pres].

Drumochter

Inverness-shire (*Druy[m] ochtyr* in c. 1591) [drʌmoxtər]

This is a name of Gaelic origin: Druim Uachdair 'upland ridge' [drəm uuəxkər], representing one of the highest areas of non-mountainous ground in Scotland.

A line of poetry sums up an attitude about this place: *'S mòr a b'fheàrr leam bhi an Druim Uchdair, na bhi an Gàidhig nan creag gruamach* 'I'd much rather be in Drumochter than be in Gaick of the frowning crags'. Gaick is a nearby place.

Duck Bay

Argyll

Duck Bay is a modern name, denoting a small bay on the south west side of Loch Lomond. This small cove was apparently unnamed until the 1960s.

Dufftown

Moray

Dufftown is a modern settlement and was founded in 1817 by James Duff, the fourth Earl of Fife (1776–1857) after whom the town is named. See also **Craigduff**.

Dumbarton

Dumbartonshire (*Dumbretan* in 1290–91) [dʌmbartən]

Although this sounds English, the name is from the Gaelic Dùn Breatann 'the fort of (the) Britons', denoting the one-time fort of the Strathclyde Britons. Somewhat to the north of Dumbarton is a stone called Clach nam Breatann 'the stone of the Britons' likely denoting the northern limit of their territory.

Dumbuck

Dunbartonshire (*Dunbuck hill* in c. 1591) [dʌmbʌk]

This is named after a place very close to **Littlemill** Distillery where this whisky was briefly produced. Names beginning with Dun- in Scotland generally come from Gaelic *dùn* 'fort'. The original fort was most likely on, or the same thing as, what is called Dumbuck Hill, although this has now been quarried away. The name is from Gaelic Dùn Buic 'buck fort' [duun buck], a *buck* being a male deer.

Dumbuck was famous in Highland Legend as a fairy hill. Thomas the Rhymer is a sort of medieval folk hero about whom many stories were invented, such as that he was abducted to fairyland and on his return was able to tell the future. In other legends, Thomas is sleeping under a hill, waiting for some future time. One version related that someone entered Dumbuck to find Thomas the Rhymer sitting up asking 'is it time?'.

Dumeath

Aberdeenshire (*Dunmeth* in 1266) [dʌmeth]

This probably reflects Gaelic Dùn Meath. *Dùn* means 'a fort', but the meaning of Meath is unknown.

Dunadd

Argyll (*Duin Att* in 683) [dʌnad]

This fort was an important site in antiquity. In modern Gaelic, the form is Dùn Ad. *Dùn* means 'a fort', but the meaning of *Ad* is unknown, despite several suggestions, none of which fit linguistically. In all likelihood, it comes from an earlier Pictish name of unknown provenance.

DÙN

Gaelic *dùn*, often anglicized as Dun-, is a very common element in Gaelic toponymy. Originally it denoted the site of a hill-fort, but latterly came to be applied to any hill that would be suitable for a fort, i.e. a protuberance with steep sides and a flat top, that often overlooks the surrounding area. It is commonest in Perthshire and Argyll.

Dunaverty

Kintyre, Argyll (*obsessio Aberte* in 712) [dʌnaverti]

This name is of Gaelic origin, from Dùn Àbhartaidh 'the fort of Àbhartach' [duun avərshti]. It is not clear who Àbhartach was, but there is an Irish story of a dwarf magician with this name who lived in Slaghtaverty (which also contains the personal name) in Derry, Ireland.

Dun Bheagan

Skye (*Dunvegane* in 1541) [dun vekan]

This is the Gaelic spelling of a place on Skye which is called Dunvegan in English. It is properly spelled Dùn Bheagan 'Beagan's fort' where Beagan is a male personal name. It has nothing to do with the dietary lifestyle. There is a Gaelic saying: *Chaidh tu gu Dùn Bheagan orm*, literally 'you went to Dunvegan on me' which is used when someone goes to the extreme or takes things too far.

Duncraggan

Stirlingshire (*Drumcragane* in 1451)

There is a place in Stirlingshire called Duncraggan, although this whisky is a blend so we cannot be sure if this place was meant to be denoted. Duncraggan in Stirlingshire is a Gaelic name. A few hundred years ago, it was probably Druim a' Chreagain 'the ridge of the little crag' [drim ə xrekin] and it was later changed to something like Dùn a' Chreagain 'the fort of the little crag' [dun ə xrekin]. Such changes are quite common.

Duncraig

Inverness-shire (*Cragy* in 1548)

Assuming this name has not been invented to sound Scottish, it might be coined from Duncraig Castle at Plockton. In Gaelic, this was simply known as A' Chreag 'the crag' [ə xrek]. The older name for the site, however, from before when the castle was built, was Am Fasadh Àlainn 'the beautiful dwelling' [əm fasagh aaliñ].

The Dundee

Dundee City (*Donde* in twelfth century) [dʌn<u>di</u>]

This name originally denoted 'the fort of the Tay', although the second element has changed a great deal over time – the modern Gaelic form for the river Tay is Tatha. The 'fort' in question is likely to be the hill known as Dundee Law. Various Latin forms of the name exist, such as *Taodunum*, (which could contain the word *dùn* and a form of *Tatha* or Tay) but it is not clear whether or not they reflect genuine early forms.

In recent times, this city is often referred to as Dùn Dè [dun jee] in Gaelic, as though it meant 'the fort of God', although of course this is fanciful; traditionally the form Dùn Deagh [dun jaw] was more popular and is still used by many today.

Dunglas

Dunbartonshire (*Dunglas* in 1550)

This is named after a place very close to **Littlemill** Distillery, where this whisky was briefly produced. It appears on maps as Dunglass and is from An Dùn Glas 'the grey/green fort' [ən dun glas]. Dunglass Castle now stands here, on a promontory jutting out into the River Clyde, an excellent location for a fort. Apparently the single -s is due to a misspelling in cask documents.

Dunhill

There are two places in Scotland called Dun Hill (with two words): one in Galloway and another near Aberfeldy. These both probably simply come from Gaelic An Dùn 'the fort' [ən duun]. When English took over in these areas, the word *hill* was added as an extra explanation. Whether either of these two places is connoted in the name of this whisky is unknown, however.

Dunhillion

This was a limited range produced by Dunhill, so it seems this name is Dunhill with -ion added, perhaps on analogy with the name Schiehallion.

Dun Naomhaig

See **Dunnyveg**.

Dunnottar

Aberdeenshire (*Dúinfoither* in 681) [dʌnotər]

This was a well-known site in antiquity, which is mentioned many times in the Irish annals. The name was originally Pictish, and was then adopted into Gaelic as Dùn Fhoithir [dun oi-ər]. *Dùn* means 'fort' and *Foithir* is an Old Gaelic word seen in several place-names meaning a 'terraced slope'. See also **Dunadd**.

Dunnyveg / Dunyvaig / Dun Naomhaig

Islay (*Dounnovaige* in 1545) [dʌn nivik / dun nw̃vik]

These three names are all variant spellings of the same place on Islay. The first two forms are anglicisations of the Gaelic form, which is represented by the third form. This would be better spelled Dùn Naomhaig [dun nw̃vik], which means 'the fort of (Saint) Naomhag'. Naomhag, or earlier Naomhoc, was a male saint who is also seen in the name of Kilmonivag in Lochaber.

Dun Mhor

There is no such place-name in Scotland. It looks to be a combination of Gaelic *dùn* 'fort' and *mòr* 'large', although written with the *h* in Mhor it is not grammatical Gaelic. See 'the Ghaelic h' on p. 30.

Dunosdale

Skye (*Oysestill* in 1541) [dʌnosdeil]

This is a place very near Dunvegan on Skye. The name is now written as Dùn Osdale on maps. Nearby is a settlement called Osdale, therefore the name Dun Osdale name means 'the fort of Osdale', where Gaelic *dùn* is added to the existing name. Osdale is from Gaelic Osdal, which itself is from Norse, containing *dalr* 'valley', likely denoting the course of the present Glen Osdale.

Duntreath

Dunbartonshire (*Duntreith* in 1499) [dʌntriith]

Duntreath is from Gaelic *dùn* 'hill-fort', with an obscure second element.

Dunwoodie

Dunwoodie is the name of a blended Scotch made specifically for American audiences. It is bottled by a 'Montague Co in NY, NY' which makes it likely that this was named after the Dunwoodie district of Yonkers, in New York. This district is likely coined from the surname Dunwoodie, which derives from two places in Scotland, now called Dinwoodie. Both these names are most likely Brittonic in origin from a *dīn wï:δjo* 'hill-fort of the wooded place'.

Dunyvaig

See **Dunnyveg**.

Easan Biorach

See **Glen Eason**.

Ebenezer Place

Caithness

This name commemorates a street in Wick in Caithness which is the smallest street in the United Kingdom, as recognised by the Guinness Book of Records in 2006. The majority of streets in this area were named after people connected in some way with the British Fisheries Society, an organisation that heavily developed the town. Most likely the original Ebenezer was a family member of someone connected with the Society.

Eden Mill
Fife

This means 'the mill of the River Eden'; the Eden is an extensive river in Fife, which flows into the sea just north of St Andrews. Although this river-name does not relate to the Garden of Eden, it is nonetheless an ancient name.

Despite a number of suggestions, the original meaning of the name is unclear. It was possibly recorded in the second century AD by Ptolemy, an Egyptian geographer, as *Tina*. It is far from clear, however, if this really represents the Eden, or if it represents an earlier name for the river, or even if it is a miscopying of an earlier form. There are several rivers with the same name in the British Isles.

Edradour
Perthshire (*Edderdedowar* in 1509)

The name Edradour is from an older Gaelic name Eadar Dà Dhobhair [eter daa ghower] meaning broadly 'between the two waters' In modern Gaelic, the name is Eadra Dhobhair [etra ghowər]. The two rivers are now called Kinnaird Burn and The Black Spout or Edradour Burn, but in Gaelic they were known as Allt Dobhar Shuas 'upper burn of Dobhar' [auLt dower huəs] and Allt Dobhar Shìos 'lower burn of Dobhar' [auLt dowər hii-əs] respectively. This is an excellent place for a distillery. At the foot of the Black Spout is a pool in the river called Poll Dobhair 'the pool of Dobhar'.

Dobhar is an old word for 'water' which is no longer in use in modern Gaelic but here is really used as the name for the watercourse. *Dobhar* in modern Gaelic means 'otter' in Gaelic, in the sense of a creature that lives in water, although this is not the meaning here as has been claimed. This is paralleled by the English word *otter* which is related to the word *water*.

Eilean Dhubh

This seems to be a fabricated name. In Gaelic, it broadly means 'black island' from *eilean* 'island' and *dubh* 'black'. There are several places in Scotland with this name, but they are spelled (An t-)Eilean Dubh (without the h) rather than as Dhubh, which is not grammatical. See p. 30.

See p. 30.

Eileandour

There is no such place as this in Scotland. The blurb on the back of the bottle says Eileandour is Gaelic for 'Island Water'. It is not. Whilst it is true that *eilean* is Gaelic for 'island', and that some anglicised names with -dour in them (such as Aberdour and Edradour) derive from an old word *dobhar* meaning 'water'. The order of the words is not correct for the meaning of 'island water'.

Eilean Na Hearadh

Western Isles

This is a sort of Gaelic form of 'the Isle of Harris', although it is not generally referred to as such in Gaelic. See **Isle of Harris** for more details.

Eilan Gillan

There is no such place-name as this in Scotland. The first element appears to be a misspelling of Gaelic *eilean* 'island', whilst the second element might be Gaelic *gillean* 'boys, servants'. Alternatively, the second element could be the surname.

Elgin

See **Old Elgin**.

Ellisland

Dumfries (*Alizland* in 1304)

This is another whisky in the Robert Burns Collection and commemorates the house that Robert Burns built in 1788. This name is of Scots origin, probably from the female personal name *Alice* plus *land*.

The Eriskay

Western Isles (*Eriskay* in 1549)

Eriskay is an island in the Western Isles, famous for an event in 1941 when the SS Politician ran aground, depositing forty thousand bottles of whisky on the island. The name is of Old Norse origin: *Eriksøy* meaning 'Eric's Isle', passing into Gaelic as Èirisgeigh [eerishkai].

Falkirk

Stirlingshire (*egglesbreth* in c. 1120)

This name is of British origin, likely originally meaning 'the speckled church'. In the Gaelic era, the name was translated as An Eaglais Bhreac, of the same meaning and using cognate elements. Gaelic *eaglais*, and its British equivalent, are loan words from Latin *ecclesia* 'church', whilst *breac* means 'speckled'.

The modern name Falkirk is an early translation of the Gaelic or British form into Scots 'faw kirk' of the same meaning. The -l- has crept in due to hypercorrection, since in Scots a syllable final -l is sometimes dropped (such as Scots *ba'* for English *ball*).

Fascadale

Ardnamurchan, Lochaber (*Fascadal* in 1750) [faskədail]

There are two Fascadales in Scotland, one is a bay on the north coast of Ardnamurchan, the other one is in Knapdale just south of Lochgilphead. The first one is known in Gaelic as Faisgeadal [fashkatəl] whilst the latter has a slightly different form: Fasgadal [faskatəl]. Both these names are of Norse origin, containing some obscure element followed by *dalr* 'valley'.

Fellsglen

This is a fabricated name; the whisky is made by a company called John Fells & Son, so presumably, the name comprises the surname Fells, followed by the 'whisky glen' (see p. 68).

Ferintosh

Ross and Cromarty (*Iern tosh* in 1654, probably supposed to be *Fern tosh*.)

A hundred years ago, this name was known in Gaelic as An Tòiseachd [ən tooshoxk] 'the Thaneship', but the English forms seems to be taken from an earlier Gaelic form: Fearann an Tòiseachd 'the lands of the Thaneship' [ferəN ən to̲o̲shoxk]. A thane was a noble who held land from the king, and in 1476 this land, along with others, was granted to William the Thane of Cawdor, giving it the name.

Fettercairn

Aberdeenshire (*Fethirkern* in 1359)

Locally this was pronounced a century or so ago as Farcairn. The first part of this name is from Gaelic *foithir* 'slope' [foyər]. *Foithir* is made up of two words *fo* 'under' and *tìr* 'land' [tchiir]. It may, however, be adapted from an earlier Pictish word like **uotir*, of the same meaning. See **Dunnotter**.

The second part is from a Pictish element **carden*, an element of uncertain meaning, but one which appears often in Scotland, in names such as Kincardine. (See also **Pluscarden** and **Urquhart Castle**.) Some sources say that this name means 'foot of the mountain', perhaps from a folk-etymology of the name as 'foot o' cairn', but this is not true.

The burn which flows past the distillery is called Burn of Cauldcots, coined from the nearby Cauldcots Farm. This is Scots for 'cold cottages', indicating that the farm is in an exposed location.

Finlaggan

Islay (insula Sancti *Finlagani* in 1427)

The English name Finlaggan sounds as if it is from Gaelic Am Fionn Lagan 'the little white hollow' [əm fyuuN lakan], and this, or something very similar, is given as the Gaelic form for MV Finlaggan, the ferry which sails between Kennacraig and Islay.

The name, however, has never been recorded as such on Islay, where a continuous Gaelic tradition has existed since the time of the Lordship of the Isles. The form Loch Bhìollagain [lox viiLəkin] was recorded a century ago, which probably reflects a saint's name, Findlugán. The early form, mentioned above, is simply Latin for 'the island of Saint Findlugán'.

Locally, however, the settlement is referred to as Port an Eilein 'the port of the island' [porsht ən elin] with the loch being Loch (Phort) an Eilein 'the loch (of the port) of the island' [lox (forsht) ən elin].

Finnieston

Glasgow

This district of Glasgow was named in the eighteenth century after a Rev. Mr Finnie, tutor or chaplain to a Mr Anderson of Stobcross, the founder of Anderston and Finnieston. Supposedly, some handloom weavers gave it the nickname 'the world's end' because of the poor conditions there.

Fleet Street

This Scotch was sold to American audiences but had an English place-name. Fleet Street (*Fletestrete* in 1272) is, of course, a famous location in London, the street is named after the River Fleet which has long since been covered over. The name comes from Old English *flēot* 'an inlet or creek'.

Fochabers

Moray (*Fochober* in 1150–53)

This is a name of unclear derivation. The final -abers may be the same word as the Pictish *aber-* although this is far from certain. See p. 1.

Fogwatt

Moray (*Fogwett Moss* in 1871)

The derivation of this name is far from clear. There appear to be two places with a similar name, the moss and a small settlement nearby. Most likely this is a name of Scots origin, from *fog* 'moss' and *wat* 'wet' thus 'wet moss' which described the place very well.

Foinaven

Sutherland (*Bin Finnevin* in c. 1591)

The name of this mountain is from Gaelic Foinebheinn [fonyə-veiñ]. This may be from Gaelic 'wart-hill' or may be from an earlier Norse derivation, altered by folk-etymology into the Gaelic meaning.

Friar's Carse

Dumfries (*Freirhauch* in 1565)

This whisky is part of the Robert Burns Collection, and all the whiskies relate to places connected with his life. Burns lived near Friar's Carse in Dumfries. The name is Scots, a *friar* is a type of monk, and a *carse* is a 'stretch of land beside a river'. The early form *Freirhauch*, mentioned above, contains Scots *haugh* instead of *carse*. The two words have very similar meanings.

Fuaran Ile

There is no evidence this is a real place, but, as Fuaran Ìle it is Gaelic for 'the spring or well of Islay' [fuəran iiĺə]. See **Caol Ila**.

Gairloch

Ross and Cromarty (*Garloch* in 1566) [gairlox]

This is from Gaelic Geàrrloch 'short loch' [gyaarlox]. The actual location of the loch is not obvious to visitors today but it has been established locally as being a well at the mouth of (An) Abhainn Ghlas 'the grey river' [ən aviñ ghlas].

Garnheath

North Lanarkshire (*Garnhigh* in 1801) [garnhiith]

The origin of this name is unclear, although it is most likely Gaelic. Most probably it represents Gart na h-Àtha 'the enclosure of the kiln' [garsht nə haa]. Gaelic *gart* 'enclosure' appears in several other names in the area.

The Gauldrons

Kintyre, Argyll

This name, which denotes a stretch of beach to the south of Machrihanish, is also spelled Galdrings and Galdrans. Marked on Ordnance Survey maps nearby is a place called Eudan nan Gallan, which looks to be what would be spelled in modern Gaelic as Aodann nan Gallan meaning 'the hill-face of the storms' or perhaps 'of the standing stones' [wtan nan gauLan]. Another form from the late eighteenth century is the name Unan Gallan, which likely represents Innean (or Aonan) nan Gallan. *Innean* has several meanings in place-names, though it is not used in modern Gaelic. Here it is perhaps best interpreted as 'rock'.

The question remains though of whether this Gaelic name – whatever the form – represents the name the Gauldrons. One estate map gives Geal-tràigh 'white beach' as a form of the name, but whether this represents a *bonafide* form of the Gauldrons, or is merely an opinion of the author is not known.

Gerston

Caithness (*Greynstane* in 1538)

This name is of Germanic origin, either from Scots *gray-stane* 'grey stone' or possibly from Norse *Geirrstaðr* 'Geirr's farm', where *Geirr* is a personal name.

Girvan

Ayrshire (*Innirgarvan* in 1253)

The name Girvan is Gaelic in origin; the early form above represents what would be written in modern Gaelic as Inbhir Gharbhain 'the confluence of the River Girvan' [inyər gharavin]. Several other places around Scotland are or were named with *inbhir* (see p. 1). Inverness or Gaelic Inbhir Nis means 'the confluence of the River Ness'. See also **Strathayr** for discussion of the name Ayr, which has a parallel evolution.

The name of the River Girvan itself comes from Gaelic Garbhan 'rough one'. *Garbh* [garav] means 'rough' and is often applied to describe rivers.

Glamis Castle

Angus (ecclesia de *Glamenes*' 1250–59) [glams]

The castle relates to the settlement Glamis here, which is in Gaelic called Glamas [glaməs]. The meaning of the name is unknown; possibly it could mean 'place of the cries or noises' but this is a guess.

The Scots words *glen* 'valley and *ben* 'mountain' come from Gaelic words *gleann* and *beinn* respectively, with the same meanings. There is a well-known Gaelic saying about the Highlands: *Tìr nam Beann, Tìr nan Gleann, Tìr nan Gaisgeach* 'land of bens, land of glens, land of heroes'.

In terms of marketing, it seems that the most important quality of a Scotch whisky name is to sound authentically Scottish. To that end, certain words have become markers that make a browser (often unconsciously) understand the Scottishness of the product they are perusing. Thus, various words are often attached to the name. The most commonly used word in this context is glen-; in fact, very few of the Scotches called 'Glen something' actually derive from a *bonafide* place-name. In the majority of cases, the word has been added to a pre-existing place, a personal name, a surname, a random word, or even a nonsense word. This has also happened to a lesser extent with other elements such as Ben, Inver and Strath.

In 2019 the Scotch Whisky Association won a court battle with German distillery Waldhorn over their usage of the word 'glen' in the name of their whisky Glen Buchenbach. (Buchenbach is a valley in Germany.) It was proven to the court's satisfaction that the word 'glen' was sufficiently uniquely Scottish enough that the word was deemed to be misleading when used in the name of a whisky not produced in Scotland.

Gleann Banbh

This is a Gaelic form of the 'whisky glen' see above) using the Gaelic Gleann instead of the usual Glen. Although no such place as this exists in Scotland, Banbh is the Gaelic form of **Banff**.

Gleesdale

This is a fabricated place-name. Many names in Scotland end in -dale (see p. 48).

Glen Adam

This is the 'whisky glen' (see p. 68) with the personal name Adam added. The reason for the use of this personal name is unknown.

Glenaden

Aberdeenshire

This distillery, which was operational from 1845 to 1915, may be the earliest example of the 'whisky glen' (see p. 68). Glenaden Distillery was the property of a J. Russell Esq. of Aden, a small estate on the other side of Old Deer, after which this distillery was named. The derivation of Aden [adən] is unclear but it was spelled *Alnedene* 1324–1430. The original elements appearing in this name are not clear, but likely the word *allt* 'burn, stream' is involved somehow.

Glen Afton

East Ayrshire (*Ichtonn* fl in c. 1591 for Afton Water)

Glen Afton is in East Ayrshire and the Afton Water runs through it. This river-name is obscure in origin, we cannot even be sure what language it comes from. Earlier sources give the name as *Achton* or *Ichton* which strongly suggests the final syllable in the name does not contain Scots *tun* 'town'. Many old Celtic river-names end in a similar suffix, so this name might be from that stratum.

Glen Albyn

Inverness-shire

The Great Glen of Scotland runs through the centre of the country, from Fort William to Inverness, in which Loch Ness sits. It is known in Gaelic as Gleann Mòr na h-Albainn 'the great glen of Scotland' [glauN mor nə halepiñ] or simply as An Gleann Mòr 'the great glen' [ən glauN mor]. Ordnance Survey maps call this Glen Albyn, but this spelling of Albyn seems to be based on a confusion between two distinct words. The first is Albainn, a form of Alba, the Gaelic name for Scotland. The second word is the distinct personal name Alpin, best known in the name Kenneth MacAlpin, a semi-historical first King of Scots, his descendants were called the Clan Alpin.

The word Albainn also appears in the name Breadalbane, which is in Gaelic Bràghad Albainn 'the ridge of Scotland' [braad aləpiñ].

See also **Glen Mhor**.

Glenallachie

[glen aləxi]

Glenallachie is not a real name but is comprised of the 'whisky glen' plus Allachie. Allachie is a nearby name, which is applied to the Wood, Knock and Burn of Allachie. It comes from Gaelic *Eileachaidh* meaning originally a rocky place. It can mean a water channel in modern Gaelic. Thus, the tagline of this whisky 'Valley of the rocks' is not far wrong. See also **Craigellachie**.

Glen Aln

This was produced and bottled by the Alnwick Rum Company Limited. The River Aln flows into the sea at a place called Alnwick which simply means 'the farm on the River Aln' in Old English. There is no Glen Aln, although such a place-name would be topographically appropriate. It is the 'whisky glen' added (see p. 68) to the existing river-name. The Aln is an old Celtic river-name.

Glen Ardoch

Perthshire (aquis de… *Ardochie* in 1662)

There is no such place as this in Scotland, although there are several places called Ardoch. This blend was made by the **Deanston** Distillery, so it seems sensible that the nearby Ardoch Burn was intended. The name Ardoch is from Gaelic Àrdach 'high place' [arshtox]. This then has the 'whisky glen' added (see p. 68).

Glen Argyll

This is the 'whisky glen' (see p. 68) with Argyll added; Argyll, of course, is a large region in south-west Scotland. In modern Gaelic, it is Earra Ghàidheil, and earlier was Oirthir Ghàidheal meaning 'the coast land of the Gaels', denoting the western coast of Scotland as the border of the Kingdom of the Gaels. It now represents a smaller area than it did in the past.

Glen Arvin

This is a Scotch imported into the United States by the British-American Company Ltd, based in Los Angeles. Arvin is a small city north of Los Angeles, named after an Arvin Richardson. This whisky is probably named after this place, with the 'whisky glen' (see p. 68) added.

Glen Bannock

There is no such place as this in Scotland. This name seems to be based on the existing name **Bannockburn**, with the -burn removed and the 'whisky glen' (see p. 68) added on.

Glen Bervie

Aberdeenshire / Sutherland

There are two places in Scotland called Glen Bervie, both of them named after the rivers which run through them. They are both known in Gaelic as Gleann Biorbhaidh [g̊lauN birivi]. Biorbhaidh is from Old Irish *berb* 'boil', relating to the way the river flows, as if bubbling or boiling.

Glen Blair

There is no such place-name as this in Scotland. It appears to be the 'whisky glen' (see p. 68), with Blair added. Blair is both a Scottish place-name and a personal name. As a place-name, it comes from the Gaelic word *blàr* 'field' or 'battle-field'. It also appears in the name for **Blair Atholl** and Blairgowrie.

Glenborrodale

Lochaber (Glenborgadal in 1801)

This is a Gaelic name, from Gleann Borradail, which means 'the glen of Borradal'. Whilst there is some local tradition that Borrodale was a

Norwegian chief (there is even Borrodale's Grave, marked on maps), Borradale, or Borradal as it is known in Gaelic is from Old Norse *borga-dalr* 'fort valley'. The fort in question is now called Caisteal Breac (Gaelic for 'speckled castle') [kashtchəl vreck].

Glen Broch

There is no such place-name as this in Scotland. It appears to be the 'whisky glen' (see p. 68), with the word *broch* added. A broch is a form of stone tower which was commonly built in antiquity mainly around the northern coasts of Scotland. Where the word appears in Scottish place-names, it sometimes comes from Gaelic *bruach* 'bank', such as Brochroy from Am Bruach Ruadh 'the red bank'.

Glenbrynth

There is no such place-name as this in Scotland. It appears to be the 'whisky glen' (see p. 68), with the word *brynth* added. This is the Welsh word for 'purchase', though whether this is relevant is unknown.

Glenburgie

This name is the 'whisky glen' (see p. 68) added to a place in Nairnshire called Burgie (*Burgyn* in 1229). Burgie may be Norse in origin, from *borg* 'fort', passed through Gaelic as Borgaidh and then into English as Burgie.

Glencadam

(*Caldhem* in c. 1591)

The 'cadam' part of the name is from a settlement that once existed at the site of the distillery which was known as Cauldhame, Scots for 'cold home'. The name still appears on maps as Caldhame Gardens. Again, the 'whisky glen' (see p. 68) was added to the name to make the name of the whisky.

The water source for this distillery is the River South Esk, see **Glenesk** for a discussion of that name.

Glen Calder

Calder is a common river-name in Scotland, but there is no such place in Scotland with this name. Clearly the 'whisky glen' (see p. 68) has been added on to the name Calder, and in all likelihood, there is no particular Calder in mind. Calder is also a surname, so it may be coined from a person with that name. Calder as a river-name is from an Old Celtic root *caleto-dubron* 'hard water'.

Glen Carron

Ross and Cromarty (Loch Carron is *Loghcarn* in 1275)

Glen Carron in Ross-shire is named after the River Carron which flows through it; it is also fed by Loch Carron (in Gaelic Loch Carrann). There are several rivers so named in Scotland. The name derives from an old Celtic root *carr-* meaning something like 'rocky area', and all the River Carrons have rocky beds. There was once a proverb about the 'Carronites' or people from Glen Carron which runs:

> Cho fad 's a bhios fiodh 'sa choille, bithidh car anns a' Charrannach.

> As long as there is wood in the forest, there will be fraud in the Carronites.

This is a pun on the word *car* 'fraud' and the name of Carron.

Glen Catrine

Ayrshire

Catrine is a place-name in Ayrshire, with Glen attached. Catrine is possibly a Pictish or early Gaelic root from *ceit* meaning 'dark or gloomy place'. Loch Katrine in Stirlingshire (which is the source for the Auchentoshan Distillery) probably has the same derivation. In both cases, the name has been reanalysed as the female personal name.

Glen Clova

Angus (*Clovay* in 1527)

The name Glen Clova is from Gaelic Gleann Chlabhaidh [glauN xlavi]. Glens are usually named after their rivers, but in this case Clova is a settlement in the glen, and the river which runs through it is called River South Esk in English. The name of the settlement in Gaelic is Clabha [klavə], of uncertain meaning.

Glen Clyde

There is no such place as Glen Clyde, the course of the River Clyde is Strathclyde, broadly speaking. See **Glen** on p. 68 and **Strathclyde** for a discussion of the name of the Clyde.

Glencoe

Lochaber (*Glencowyn* in 1500)

This famous name has two Gaelic forms depending on what place is denoted. The name of the actual glen itself (written Glen Coe as two words) is Gleann Comhann [ḡlauN kō-əN]. *Comhann* is the name of the river here, but its meaning is unknown. The Gaelic name of the village – spelled as a single word Glencoe – is known in Gaelic as A' Chàrnaich meaning 'the stoney place or place of cairns' [ə xaarnic] from the Gaelic word *càrn* 'cairn'.

Glen Coulmony

Nairnshire (*Cheulmony* in c. 1591) [kulmoni]

This is the 'whisky glen' (see p. 68) added to the name of the real settlement of Coulmony on the River Findhorn. Coulmony is a Gaelic name, probably from Cùil a' Mhonaidh 'the nook of the moor' [kuul ə voni], although we cannot be certain.

Glencraig

Glencraig is not a real place but has the 'whisky glen' (see p. 68), and is named after Hiram Walker's production director, Willie Craig.

Glen Crinan

(*Kantracrenane* in 1480 for Ceann Tràigh a' Chrìonain 'the beach end of Crinan')

This has the 'whisky glen' (see p. 68) added to the pre-existing name Crinan, most commonly known in the name of the Crinan Canal. This is in Gaelic An Crìonan [ən krǖǐənan] which likely has something to do with the word *crìon* 'small, withered' possibly meaning 'withered place'.

Glen Darbach

There is no such place as this in Scotland. It appears to contain the 'whisky glen' (see p. 68), alongside the word Darbach. This word is unknown in Scotland either as a place-name or a word. The name does appear in Germany as a river-name and also as a surname, but whether there is any German connection is unknown.

Glendarroch

Argyll [glendarox]

Glendarroch is at the foot of a burn called Kilduskland Burn; one source, however, calls this burn 'The Darroch', so in all likelihood the glen through which it ran was called Glen Darroch. The name most likely comes from Gaelic Gleann an Daraich 'the glen of the oak(s)' [glauN ən daric]. A mile or so to the north of this site are two places: Auchendarroch and Oakfield. These are two names meaning the same thing, one in Gaelic and one in English.

It is worth noting that the source of the Kilduskland Burn is a small loch originally called Loch na h-Inghinn 'the loch of the girl' [lox ne heē-iñ] in Gaelic. By the time of the second edition of the Ordnance Survey in 1898 however, the name had been changed to 'The Still Loch', a Scots name clearly referring to the distillery.

Glen Deer

Aberdeenshire (*Deár* c. 1130)

There is no such place as Glen Deer, but Deer is the name of a parish in Aberdeenshire. This name likely comes from an Old Gaelic *dair* meaning 'oak grove', the modern word for this being *doire* [dʌrə]. Deer is famous to Gaelic scholars because it was here that an early Gaelic manuscript, The Book of Deer, was written. This book gives a founding legend for the name of Deer; it relates that a saint called Drostan, when he was leaving his master Columba, was so sad that a tear fell from his cheek, so Columba said 'Let *déar* (Gaelic for 'tear') be its name from now on'.

It should also be remarked that the label for this whisky depicts a deer's head, so it may simply be that the animal is meant here, with no reference to the existing place-name.

Glen Demort

The tagline for this whisky is 'The Whisky that must not be named', suggesting a horror theme, thus the French phrase *de mort* 'of death' might be meant here as a joke, as if meaning 'Glen of death'.

ILLICIT WHISKY DISTILLING IN SCOTTISH PLACE-NAMES

Given that whisky distilling – both legal and illegal – was such a huge industry, it is perhaps strange that this has not left a more pronounced mark on Scottish place-names. It may be that because the industry is relatively modern – only a few hundred years old –that there has not been so much time for changes to have been recorded on maps. The following names, however, are a few examples of evidence for illicit distilling as seen in place-names in the Highlands.

In Newtonmore, there is a small burn which runs into the Spey called **Caochan na Staile** 'the distillery burn' [k̲wxan nə stalə]. Nearby are two hills: **Tom na Mòine** 'the peat hill' [tom ne moñə] and **Cnoc a' Ghuail** 'the coal hill' [kroxk ə ghu-il], perhaps relating to two substances used in the distilling process.

High up in Sutherland, near the source of the River Helmsdale, there are two nearby place-names which clearly relate to the days of illicit whisky distilling: **Cnoc Bothan Uisge-Beatha** and **Allt Bothan Uisge-Beatha** meaning respectively 'hill' and 'burn' 'of the whisky bothies'.

In Kintyre, just south of Muasdale is **Uamh Bealach a' Chaochain** 'the cave of the pass of the wash' (wash in the sense of whisky in its first process of distillation). This cave has an excellent spring of water and was a suitable place to make and smuggle whisky from.

In the Lowlands, there are several names such as **Whisky House**, **Whisky Sike** in Roxburghshire, or **Whisky Hope** in Selkirkshire, all denoting illicit whisky distilling.

Left: This new bottling of Allt a' Bhainne uses the meaning of 'Milk Burn' as a visual joke on its label.

(Reproduced with the permission of That Boutique-y Whisky Company).

Below: Kelso Abbey from Kelso Abbey by Frederick Christian Lewis, drawn by W. Wilson (1809).

(flickr.com/photos/britishlibrary/50263993161/).

Top: Campbeltown Loch, with Kilkerran on the opposite shore, and Ben Guillion in the background with its 'shoulders' from *Select Views on the River Clyde (1830)* by J. Fleming (died 1845). (flickr.com/photos/britishlibrary/11007656616).

Above: A bilingual train station sign.

Opposite page, from top: *The Twa Brigs: The Auld Brig and New Brig* from *Scotland Illustrated in a Series of Views taken expressly for this work (1838)* by W. Beattie 1793–1875. This picture by W. H. Bartlett (1809-1854).

Sign for Drumochter Pass, known in Gaelic as Druim Uchdair (Photograph © Oliver Dixon (cc-by-sa/2.0) , geograph.org. uk/p/5892469).

Edradour Burn and Distillery. This was known as Allt Dobhar Shìos in Gaelic, whilst Edradour is from Gaelic Eadra Dhobhair 'between two burns'.

Opposite page, from top: A bilingual road sign on Islay

(Photograph © Rossographer (cc-by-sa/2.0); Source: https://www.geograph.org. uk/photo/550788, Attribution: https://creativecommons.org/licenses/by-sa/2.0).

Dalaruan from Argyll's Highlands (1902)
(archive.org/details/argyllshighlands1902bede/page/178).

The Sound of Isla from Blaeu 1654. This is the Sound of Islay', with Islay at the bottom end of the map. On the far left one can see Kyles Yla, this is from Caolas Ìle a variant form of Caol Ìle. On the right hand side is the English form of the name 'The Sound of Yla'. Lofset is Lossit and Bin bam may be a corrupted version of Bunnahabhain.

(Reproduced with the permission of the National Library of Scotland).

Below: Castle Urquhart on Loch Ness from In the Hebrides by Constance Frederica "Eka" Gordon-Cumming (died 1924).
(flickr.com/photos/britishlibrary/11162806936).

The well of Tobermory.
Tobermory or Tobar Mhoire
means '(Virgin) Mary's Well'
(cc-by-sa/2.0 - © Gordon Hatton -
geograph.org.uk/p/1818913).

Upper left: The Linlithgow Burch Crest showing the 'Black Dog'
referred to in the Gaelic form for Linlithgow

(Courtesy David B. Appleton: http://blog.appletonstudios.
com/2017/12/burgh-arms-in-and-about-st-michaels.html).

Right: Dunaverty from Glencreggan: or, A Highland
Home in Cantire (1861) by Cuthbert Bede p. 117

(Illustrations by the author, pseudonym of Edward Bradley 1827–1889;
archive.org/details/glencregganorhig01bede/page/116)

Below: Culzean Castle with Ailsa Craig in the background. From Select
Views on the River Clyde (1830) by J. Fleming (died 1845).

(flickr.com/photos/britishlibrary/11007834285).

ILA INSVLA,
ex Æbudarum majoribus una.

THE YLE OF ILA,
being one of the biggest of the Westerne Yles.

Above: Kenmore on Loch Tay (1813) by F. C. Lewis 1779–1856.
(flickr.com/photos/britishlibrary/50263997726).

Opposite page from top: The bridge at Coylumbridge.
(Photograph © Jim Barton (cc-by-sa/2.0), geograph.org. uk/p/3510443).

Finlaggan Castle from Ordnance Gazetteer
of Scotland vol v, 1884, artist unknown.
(archive.org/details/ordnancegazette01unkngoog/page/n20).

The Isle of Islay title plate from Blaeu's Atlas Novus 1654.
(Reproduced with the permission of the National Library of Scotland).

Lochnagar from The Scenery of the Dee, with pen and pencil.
Picture by Andrew Gibb (1884).

Above: Ardgowan from Modern Athens (1829)
illustrated by Thomas Hosmer Shepherd (1793–1864).

Opposite page from top: A bilingual Forestry Commission sign on the Isle of Arran
(courtesy Alasdair MacCaluim www.flickr.com/photos/amaccaluim/5837043153).

Brodick Bay from Classic Scenes in Scotland,
by modern artists by William Ballingall (1840–1919).
(flickr.com/photos/britishlibrary/11109395914).

Dunottar Castle from Ordnance Gazetteer of Scotland vol ii, 1883. (From Slezer's
Theatrum Scotiae (1693) redrawn by P. Justyne (1812–1883))
(archive.org/details/ordnancegazettv200groo/page/n15).

Tobar a' Ghàirdein 'the well of the hill', the source of the Teaninich Distillery.
Courtesy of Eilidh Scammell

*Loch Ranza with its castle. (Photograpy 1865
by Scottish photographer J. Valentine, 1815–1879.*

*(Reproduced under the Getty's Open Content Program
https://www.getty.edu/art/collection/object/104DTA).*

*Loch Lomond (1797) by Francis Jukes 1745–1812.
(flickr.com/photos/britishlibrary/50264217857).*

Glen Deveron

Moray

This name has the 'whisky Glen' (see p. 68) added to an old river-name the Deveron. See **Deveron**.

Glendorris

There is no such place as this in Scotland. It appears to be the 'whisky glen' (see p. 68) added to the personal name Dorris.

Glendouglas

Argyll (*Glen Douglash* in c. 1591)

Glen Douglas branches off the west banks of Loch Lomond. The glen here is named after the river which flows through it, called Douglas Water in English, and Dubhghlais 'black water' [duuLish] in Gaelic. There was more than one river flowing into Loch Lomond with this name; the other is now called Inveruglas Water, which was named after the settlement at the foot of the River Inveruglas. In Gaelic, it is Inbhir Dhubhghlais (see p. 1) meaning 'the confluence of the river called Dubhghlas' [iñər ghuuLish]. Such confusion is quite common in place-name studies. The personal name Douglas is coined from a place in Lanarkshire which has the same meaning.

Glen Downan

Moray (*Dunans* in 1747-55)

This is most likely the 'whisky glen' (see p. 68) added to the pre-existing name Downan near Glenlivet in Strathspey. Downan itself is probably from Gaelic An Dùnan 'the little fort' [ən duunan].

Glendramroc

This is not a place-name. The full name of the whisky is Glendramroc Royal Observer Corp, and it was made in commemoration of that body. Thus, it is likely the final -roc appears to reflect the acronym of ROC. Glendram perhaps is simply the 'whisky glen' (see p. 68) and Scots *dram* 'portion of whisky'.

GlenDronach

There is no real evidence for the name of the burn that flows past Glendronach Distillery prior to its foundation in 1825. Later sources say it was called 'the Dronac' which was altered into Glendronach to become the name of the distillery. Another source refers to it as 'the Dronah Burn'. If these forms are genuine, the watercourse probably contains the Gaelic word *dronn* 'ridge, back, rump' relating to some feature in the landscape. Ultimately, however, the origins of this name are unclear.

Glendrostan

This is not a place-name. Drostan is a Pictish personal name, ultimately meaning 'descendant of Drust'. See **Glen Deer**.

Glen Drumm

There is no such place-name as Glen Drumm in Scotland. It appears to be made up from the 'whisky glen' (see p. 68) and Drumm, more commonly spelled Drum in place-names, which usually derives from Gaelic *druim* 'ridge' [drim].

Glendullan

Outside Dufftown

Glendullan as a name does not strictly exist, but near Glendullan Distillery is Dullan Water. In Gaelic, this is called Uisge Dhuillean [ushkə ghuĺan]. Although *duillean* means 'spear' in Gaelic, it is likely that this name comes from an older Pictish root, perhaps connected with *tuil* 'flood'.

Gleneach

Each is the Gaelic word for 'horse' (cognate with Latin *equus*, of the same meaning) but no such place as Gleneach exists in Scotland.

Glen Eagle

The label of this blend shows a spreadeagle which suggests the bird is denoted here. Glen Eagles is, of course, a place; see **Ben Eagles**.

Glen Eason

Arran (*Quey's Glen* in 1814 a translated form)

This is a shortened form of Gleann Easan Biorach [glauN esan biəroχ], the glen that runs into the sea on Arran at Lochranza. The name is Gaelic, meaning 'the glen of Easan Biorach'. This is a difficult name to parse; *biorach* means 'sharp or pointed' which does not necessarily make sense for a waterfall. *Biorach* can also mean a 'heifer', and the 1814 form seems to be a Scots translation of 'Gleann Biorach', so the name may mean 'glen of the heifer's waterfall' or some such. See also **Easan Biorach**.

Glen Elgin

[elgin, not eljin]

This name has the obligatory 'whisky glen' (see p. 68) added to Elgin, which is a town in Scotland. See **Old Elgin** for discussion of that name.

Glen Ellis

There is no such place as this in Scotland. It is the 'whisky glen' (see p. 68) added to the personal name Ellis.

Glenesk

Angus

This whisky has been called North Esk and Highland Esk before being named Glen Esk. The distillery which produces this whisky sits on the banks of River North Esk in Kinnaber. The name Esk is one of a number of rivers with a similar name in Britain: there are various other Esks as well as Ex in Exeter and the Usk. These are a complicated set of names, and it is not clear if they all have the same root or not. The word *easg* [esk] may be related to the Gaelic word for 'fish' *iasg* [ee-ask] or to another word *easg* 'bog or fen' [esk]; alternatively, it may have nothing in origin to do with those words. The name, however, certainly passed into Gaelic as Easg, and the river was known as Uisge Easg 'the river Esk', [ushk esk] whilst the North Esk was known as Easg a Thuath [esk ə huə] of the same meaning. Glenesk itself known in Gaelic as Gleann Easg [glauN esk].

Glenfairn

There is no such place as this in Scotland, but there are several places which have -fairn as a second element, such as Drumfairn or Gartfairn. In these cases, the element generally derives from Gaelic *feàrn* 'alder'.

Glenfarclas

Moray

Glenfarclas Distillery takes its name from a nearby Tomfarclas, where the initial Tom- (from Gaelic *tom* 'hill') has been swapped for the 'whisky glen' (see p. 68). There is a nearby Glenfarclas Wood, but this is named after the distillery.

The underlying elements in the word Farclas are not certain, but one of the last generations of Gaelic speakers in the area gave the Gaelic form as Far-Chlach 'over stone' [far-xlax]. It may be, however, that this is a later reinterpretation of an earlier place-name form. The same informant also said that the old name for the site of the distillery was Loch a' Chlèirich 'the cleric's loch' [lox ə xleiric]. This is mirrored in the name of a nearby settlement called Rechlerich which is from Gaelic Ruighe a' Chlèirich 'the cleric's slope' [ruy ə xleiric].

Glen Faye

There is no such place as this in Scotland. It seems to be the 'whisky glen' (see p. 68) added to the personal name Faye. The identity of Faye, however, is unknown.

Glen Fergus

There is no such place as this in Scotland. Most likely it contains the 'whisky glen' (see p. 68) added to the personal name Fergus. This name Fergus was most likely chosen to signify perceived Scottishness for the French market.

Glenfiddich

Moray (*Fiddich W* in c. 1591, i.e. Fiddich Water)

This name comes from the Gaelic form Gleann Fithich or Fidhich [glauN fee-ic]. Gaelic-speaking locals latterly understood this to be either *fitheach* 'raven' or *fiadhach* 'rough'. *Fiadh* 'deer' too is commonly understood nowadays, and a deer even appears on the whisky bottle with the explanation: "The Valley of the Deer". Most likely, however, it is related to the Gaelic word *fiodh* 'wood, timber' [fyʌgh], thus perhaps meaning 'the wooded glen', or perhaps 'the glen of the Fithich' where Fithich means 'the wooded river'.

The water source for this distillery is the Robbie Dubh Spring, see **Balvenie**.

Glen Findlay

There is no such place as this in Scotland. It is 'whisky glen' (see p. 68) added to the personal name Findlay.

Glen Finloch

There is no such place as this in Scotland. It is 'whisky glen' (see p. 68) with the word Finloch added. This second element looks like an anglicisation of Gaelic Fionn Loch 'white ('with other meanings of 'cold' or 'holy') loch' [fyuuN lox], although there is no such place spelled in that way in Scotland.

Glen Flagler

The name Glen Flagler was not inspired by any Scottish glen, rather the distillery was named after Flagler Avenue in West Palm Beach, Florida, where Publicker's owner, Simon Neuman, owned a home. (Publicker is a company which has owned a number of distilleries in Scotland). Flagler Avenue itself was named after Henry M. Flagler, an early Florida railroad tycoon and regarded as the 'father' of Miami. See also **Inver House**.

Glen Fohdry

This whisky blend is owned by Quality Spirits International; there is no such place as this in Scotland. This company also makes Glen Fohry mentioned below. Could it be that Glen Fohdry is merely a 'dry' version of Glen Fohry?

Glen Fohry

This whisky is a blend owned by Quality Spirits International; there is no such place as this in Scotland. It seems to be the 'whisky glen' (see p. 68) added to the word Fohry. This is a surname of German origin, so it seems likely that this is what is being referenced here somehow. See also **Glen Fohdry** above.

Glen Forest

There is no such place as this in Scotland. The picture on the bottle depicts a forest, so the name would simply seem to be Glen (see p. 68) with English *forest*.

Glen Forrest

There is no such place as this in Scotland. This would appear to be simply the word Glen (see p. 68) with Forrest added on. Forrest can be a male personal name or a surname. This is not to be confused with Glen Forest or Glen Forres.

FICTIONAL SCOTCHES

Needless to say, alcohol – and Scotch in particular – appears countless times in television and cinema. Sometimes a specific brand is used, often involving sponsorship deals, but often, to avoid legal issues, whilst looking congruent, fictional brands have been invented. There are dozens of such whiskies, and usually they are effectively invisible to the casual observer. The most-used brand is Glencallan, which was created by Independent Studio Services. This has appeared in many episodes of American television, such as Grey's Anatomy, Community and Sons of Anarchy. The name Glencallan is likely taken from the name of the famous Macallan brand with the whisky 'glen' added.

Closer to home, the 1983 film Local Hero – set and filmed in the Scottish Highlands – had its own fake brand of whisky known as MacAskill Single Malt. The local pub in the film was the equally fictional MacAskill Arms.

Glen Forres

Moray (*Forais* in 1189–99)

This seems to relate to the well-known town of Forres and the 'whisky glen' added (see p. 68). This name is from Gaelic Farrais [farəsh] which is probably from an earlier stage of the language, containing *for* 'under' and *ras* 'shrub' with the meaning 'little shrubbery'.

Glen Foster

There is no such place as this in Scotland. It is the 'whisky glen' (see p. 68) added to the personal name Foster. The identity of Foster is unknown.

Glenfoyle

The original Glenfoyle was a name given to a distillery in Gargunnock which closed in 1923; the name was revived in the 1980s at a new site. The original name of Glenfoyle was invented using the 'whisky glen' (see p. 68) and possibly the second element of the name Aberfoyle. This is in Gaelic Obar Phuill, which is a name of Pictish origin, (see *Aber-* on p. 1); the second element is likely a British word related to Welsh *pwll* 'pool'.

Glen Fraser

There is no such place as this in Scotland. It is the 'whisky glen' (see p. 68) added to the personal name Fraser. The identity of Fraser is, however, unknown.

Glen Fruin

Argyll (*Glenfrone* in 1225)

This is the name of a real glen which flows into the west banks of Loch Lomond. It is from Gaelic Gleann Freòin [glauN friowin], of unknown meaning.

Glenfyne

Argyll

This is another name for Glendarroch. See **Loch Fyne** for a discussion of this name.

Glen Galwan

This is not a real place-name. Glen Galwan is a whisky made by a French supermarket chain called Carrefour, who also make a liqueur called O'Galwan. Thus, it seems sensible to conclude that the name is based on that, with the 'whisky glen' (see p. 68) added onto it. O'Galwan is marketed with an Irish image, so perhaps Galwan is supposed to be reminiscent of Galway; no such word exists otherwise.

Glen Garioch

Aberdeenshire (*Garuiach* in 1190–91) [glen geeri]

Garioch [geeri] is the name of an area in Aberdeenshire and Chapel of Garioch is a settlement within. There is, however, no such place as Glen Garioch; this is the 'whisky glen' (see p. 68). Garioch is from Gaelic Gairbheach [geriox]. A battle was fought here in 1411 by the forces of the Lord of the Isles and the Earl of Ross; in English, it is called the Battle of Harlaw, after a nearby hill. In Gaelic tradition, however, it is called Cath Gairbheach 'the battle of Garioch' [kah geriox].

The original meaning of this name is not clear, but it would seem to have something to do with Gaelic *garbh* 'rough' [garav], perhaps meaning 'rough place'.

Glen Garvie

There is no such place as this in Scotland, but there is a Garvie in Cowal in Argyll. This is from Gaelic Garbhaidh [garəvi] from *garbh* 'rough', thus meaning 'rough place'.

Glen Garvin

This name appears to be invented using the 'whisky glen' (see p. 68) and the name Garvin. In all likelihood, it is named after a Peter Garvin, the co-founder of supermarket chain Nisa. This whisky was managed by Cellars International which is a subsidiary of Nisa.

Glen Gency

There is no such place as this in Scotland. It seems to be the 'whisky glen' (see p. 68) with the word Gency added. The origin of the word Gency is not known, but this whisky was bottled for the French market, and Gency is a French surname, most notably known for Clause Ursule Gency who was a general in the French Revolution and Napoleonic wars.

Glen Ghillie

There is no such place as this in Scotland. The 'whisky glen' (see p. 68) is here. Ghillie is a common anglicised spelling of Gaelic *gille* 'boy, lad, servant' [gìlə, it is also known as Scottish English *gillie* in the sense of a 'groundsman'. For the h in the name, see p. 30.

Glengilp

Argyll

This is another name for Glendarroch Distillery. Glen Gilp is odd as it does not run into the head of the Loch Gilp as one would expect, but rather flows into the side of the loch. Gilp is better known as part of the settlement name Lochgilphead. The name Gilp is most likely from Gaelic *gilb* 'chisel', said to be from the shape of the loch.

Glenglassaugh

Aberdeenshire (*Glassach* in 1420) [glen glasox]

The primary name here is the Glassaugh River. This is from Gaelic *glasach* 'grey/green place' [glasox]. The modern spelling with -augh possibly was created on analogy with Scots *haugh* 'river-side meadow'. The 'whisky glen' (see p. 68) was added at a later date.

Glen Gordon

There is no such place as this in Scotland. It is the 'whisky glen' (see p. 68) added to the personal name Gordon.

Glengoyne

Dunbartonshire

This whisky was called Glen Guin or Glenguin but was changed to Glengoyne at a later date. Nonetheless, this appears to be another invented Glen- name, this time adapted from the nearby hill called Dumgoyne where Dum- has been swapped for Glen- (the 'whisky glen', see p. 68). The origin and meaning of the name Dumgoyne (*Dunguin hill* in c. 1591) are not clear. The first element, despite variations, is almost certainly Gaelic *dùn* 'fort' or 'fort-shaped hill'.

The whole name of Dumgoyne could represent something like an original Gaelic Dùn Gobhainn 'smith fort' [dun go-iñ] or Dùn Gaimhne 'stirk (a year-old calf) fort' [duun gainə], but we cannot know for sure. Glengoyne is said by some to mean in Gaelic 'the glen of the wild geese', but this would be Gleann nan Gèadh, and in any case is not a real place-name.

Glen Graeme

There is no such place as this in Scotland. It is the 'whisky glen' (see p. 68) added to the personal name Graeme.

Glen Grant

Moray

In 1840, former smuggling brothers John and James Grant decided to take out a licence to legally produce whisky. They called the whisky and distillery after themselves, with Glen- attached (see p. 68). The distillery sits on a watercourse called Back Burn; in a unique twist of fate, the course of this burn was given the name Glen Grant on the first Ordnance Survey maps. Thus, it seems that a fake glen- name became real over time.

Glen Green

There is no such place as this in Scotland. It appears to have been fabricated purely from the words *glen* (see p. 68) and *green*, which is possibly a surname.

Glen Grigor

This does not relate to a place as such, but is named after the company who makes it: William Grigor & Son, with the 'whisky glen' (see p. 68) added.

Glen Grouse

There is no such place as this in Scotland. It appears to be the 'whisky glen' (see p. 68), with the name of the bird added. It is possibly related to the popular Famous Grouse brand.

Glengyle

Argyll (*Glengill* in 1451)

This place-name is from Gaelic Gleann Goill meaning perhaps 'standing stone glen'. Alternatively, the glen might have been coined from the river, called in Gaelic Goill, meaning 'agitated water', which runs through it.

Glenhaven

There is no such place as this in Scotland, it is the 'whisky glen' (see p. 68) with the word *haven* added. *Haven* means a 'safe place' or a 'harbour'. Alternatively, the name could be a portmanteau name based on the name of Stonehaven.

Glen Hood

There is no such place as this in Scotland, it is the 'whisky glen' (see p. 68) with the word Hood added on; what Hood means is unknown, however.

Glen Hunter

There is no such place as this in Scotland, it is the 'whisky glen' (see p. 68) with the word Hunter added on, it is probably simply supposed to sound romantic, but perhaps it denotes a surname. This is unrelated to Hunter's Glen in Cowal.

Glenisla

Angus (*Glenylif* in 1219–46) [glen ailə]

Glenisla is the name of a glen in Perthshire through which the river Isla runs. It is from Gaelic Gleann Île, [g̃lauN iílə] which is of unknown origin, but probably different in origin from the island of Islay, as the early forms for this name end in -f, suggesting a different, unknown word.

Glen Keith

Moray (*Kethmalruf* in 1214)

This is coined from the town of Keith with the 'whisky glen' (see p. 68) added. Keith is a name of Pictish origin, from *coed* 'woods', a common element that appears in several names in Scotland. Keith is known as Cèith [keih] or Baile Chèith 'the town of Keith' [balə ceih] in Gaelic. In 1214 it was spelled as *Kethmalruf* reflecting Gaelic Cèith Maol Rubha 'Keith of Maol Rubha' [keih m̲w̲l̲ ruə]. Maol Rubha is the name of a popular Scottish saint who appears in several place-names.

Glenkinchie

East Lothian (*Kinchie Bleachfield* in 1747–55)

This distillery sits on the Kinchie Burn in East Lothian, and Little Kinchie is a settlement on it. This is most likely a Gaelic river-name in origin, perhaps the same as the Kingie in Inverness-shire which is likely from an Old Gaelic word *cingidh* 'champion' [king-gi]. The name is said by some to be from someone called de Quincey, a medieval landowner, but there is no evidence for this.

Glen Kindie

Aberdeenshire (*Glenkenety* in 1357) [glen kindi]

Glen Kindie is from Gaelic Gleann Cingidh [g̃lauN king-gi]. See **Glenkinchie** for the derivation.

Glen Kirk

There is a small place called Glenkirk in Ettrick Forest in the Scottish

Borders, but it is very unlikely that this place is referred to, given this whisky's Speyside associations. More likely this is simply the Scots words *glen* and *kirk* put together. *Kirk* is the Scots word for a church. The blurb of the whisky states '..."kirks", Old Norse and Old English for "church"', but the word is best understood as being Scots.

Glen Lairg

Sutherland (*Larg* in 1223–45)

This is a pre-existing name Lairg, with the 'whisky glen' (see p. 68) added. This is in Gaelic known as Luirg [lurik], which is a form of *lorg* 'track, way' [lorək].

Glenlanarach

There is no such place as this in Scotland. Removing the Glen-, the word *lanarach* is unknown in Gaelic or any other language.

Glen Laogh

Laogh is Gaelic for 'calf' [lwgh] and there are several places in Scotland with a name similar to this, meaning 'calf glen'. It is not clear if a specific place is intended.

Glen Leora

Islay

This is Gleann Leòra [glauN lyoora] on Islay, a glen that runs into the sea near Ardtalla. It is Gaelic, meaning 'the glen of river Leòra', although the river is now called Claggain River in English. Leòra is of Norse origin, perhaps from *Ljórá* 'smokehole river'.

This glen is mentioned in a love song. The relevant verse goes:

'S truagh nach robh mi a's mo leannan
An gleannan falaich, 's sinn fad' o dhaoin',
No 'n Gleanna Leòra a's badan ceò ann,
'S gu'n dèanainn còmhradh riut anns an fhraoch

It's a shame I was not with my darling

In secret glens, with us far from people
Or in Glen Leòra with copses of mist
And I would make conversation with you in the heather

Glenlivet

Moray (*Glen lyffet* in c. 1591)

This name is from Gaelic Gleann Lìobhaid [g̊lauN l̤ivitsh], but the word Livet name most likely dates from an earlier Pictish word perhaps meaning 'glittering' or 'shining'.

Glenlochy

Inverness-shire (*stagnum Lochdae* in 690) [glenloxi]

Lochy is a river-name which occurs several times throughout Scotland, and whilst the name Glen Lochy appears associated with other rivers, there is no Glen Lochy associated with the River Lochy which flows from Loch Lochy and spills out into the narrows at Fort William where this distillery is. Loch Lochy is referred to in a Latin text of around 690 as *stagnum Lochdae* which is explained in the text as 'the black goddess'. Whilst this is likely folk-etymology (i.e. something commonly understood but not historically truthful), it does reflect a partial truth. The explanation given is an Old Gaelic or Pictish word *loch* or *lòch* meaning 'black' with *-dae* meaning 'goddess' (cognate with words such as *divine* and so on). Whilst the 'goddess' part is indeed folk-etymology, the element *lòch* is likely the root element. In Gaelic, the River Lochy is Abhainn Lòchaidh [aviñ loxi].

Glenlogie

There are two uses of this name concerning whisky. Glenlogie was the name of a distillery which was open in the first half of the nineteenth century in Garioch in Aberdeenshire.

The earlier distillery is coined from a small place, but the name Logie appears several times locally, and an old name from the Garioch parish was Logie Durno, where Durno is a nearby place.

Glen Logie is also the name of a whisky that was made in the twentieth century. It is unlikely to have been a continuation of the previous distillery, however. Possibly this later Glenlogie was coined from a Glen Logie in Glen Prosen in Angus. Alternatively, there are several places around Scotland simply called Logie, and the name may reflect one of these with the 'whisky glen' (see p. 68) added.

This common term Logie can reflect two underlying Gaelic elements. The first is an unattested earlier Gaelic word *login meaning 'church'; the second is *lagan* 'little hollow'.

Glenlomyn

This is not a place-name, and the meaning of Lomyn is not known. It is, however, the Welsh word for 'bare', and appears to be a rare surname.

Glenlossie

Lossie is the name of a river, and although Glenlossie might be a reasonable name for the valley through which this river flows, it did not exist before the whisky or distillery was named; it is therefore an example of the 'whisky glen' (see p. 68). Like the Eden of Eden Mill, the name is likely very old, and its original meaning has long since been lost to us. It is possibly linked to the modern Gaelic word *lus* 'herb', although this is not certain at all.

Glenluig

This whisky was named after an earlier distillery founded in 1812. See under the list of lost distilleries.

Glen Luss

Argyll (*Glen Luss* in 1747–55)

Glen Luss runs into Loch Lomond at a settlement called Luss, after which the glen is named. Luss is also the name of the parish. The derivation of the name is unclear, but the Gaelic form Lus [lus] is the Gaelic word for a 'plant' or 'herb', and this is how the name is understood today. The same underlying form may exist in the names of Luce and Glenluce in Wigtownshire.

Glen Lyon

Perthshire (*Glenlyoun* in 1328)

This name of this famous Perthshire glen is most immediately from Gaelic Gleann Lìobhann [g̃lauN lii-uN]. Lìobhann or Lyon refers to the river and is probably pre-Gaelic in origin, perhaps from a root meaning 'shining'. One story, however, offers a different explanation: after a skirmish between the Campbells and the MacGregors, the MacGregors cleaned their swords in the river, which was thus renamed from its supposed original name Duibhe 'blackness': *Bho latha lìomhadh nan arm, bithidh Lìobhann mar ainm air Duibhe* 'from the day of the polishing of the weapons, Lyon will be the name of the Duibhe'. This is a pun on the word *lìomh* 'polish' [liiu] and Lìobhann.

A Gaelic proverb also relates to this glen: *Bha dà chaisteal dheug aig Fionn ann an Crom-Ghleann nan Clach* 'Fingal had twelve castles in the Crooked Glen of the Stones', this being an epithet for the glen.

Glen Mac Clay

Arran (*Glenklowy* in 1472)

This may be a version of Glen Cloy, which is from Gaelic Gleann (Mh)ac Lothaidh [g̃lauN axk lo-i], meaning 'the glen of MacLothaidh' where MacLothaidh is a surname sometimes written in English as MacCloy.

Glen Marnoch

There is no such place as Glen Marnoch; this is a whisky made from rejected barrels. There are several places called Marnoch or the like in Scotland however, but if any of these specifically coins this whisky name, or of the word was picked for marketing purposes, we cannot know. There is a place called Marnoch near Aberchirder deep in distillery territory, so it may be coined from that. This may derive from a saint's name, as seen in names such as Kilmarnock and Inchmarnock.

Glen Mhor

[glen voor]

This distillery in Inverness relates to a large glen which runs through Scotland from Inverness to Fort William, and which also contains Loch Ness. In English, it is called the Great Glen, and in Gaelic, An Gleann Mòr. This name is a version of this, with the Ghaelic h inserted, see p. 30. On Ordnance Survey maps, the glen is also called Glen Albyn, although nobody ever calls it that. See **Glen Albyn**.

Glenmorangie

Ross and Cromarty [glen mor<u>ə</u>nji]

The name Glenmorangie is perhaps the most controversial of the invented names. 'The Glen of Tranquility' was a slogan used by the company as a translation of this name, deriving it from a Gaelic 'Gleann mor na sìth'. This is alas untrue; the name derives from the place-name Morangie, with the usual 'whisky glen' (see p. 68) added on. Morangie as a name is Gaelic in origin, being Mòraistidh [m<u>o</u>rəsh-tchi] in modern Gaelic, from an earlier Mòr-innisidh meaning 'big haugh place'. *Haugh* is a word for a dry area near water.

Inventing place-names from whisky is of course nothing new, but it was perhaps inadvisable to refuse to admit the fact. As an article stated 'The company said it acknowledged the meaning of Glenmorangie depended on the "perceived root of the word" and there was an academic argument over how various Scottish place-names may have originated, but it believed the translation it had used was correct'.

The distillery's water source is in a place called Tarlogie; this is perhaps a Pictish place-name, from the elements *tal 'brow' and *arg 'silver'.

Glen Moray

[glen mʌri]

This is the well-known name Moray with the 'whisky glen' (see p. 68) added on. Moray (*Murebe* in 1032) is the name of the region in which Elgin lies. In Gaelic, it is Moireabh [mʌriv], but it derives from an earlier form *Moritreb meaning 'sea settlement'.

Glen Morgain

Glen Morgain was bottled for a German market. Morgain is similar to the word Morgan, a Gaelic personal name as well as the German word for 'morning'.

Glen Morven

There is no such place as Glen Morven, rather this is the name Morven with the 'whisky glen' (see p. 68) added. See **Ben Morven** for the discussion of Morven.

Glen Ness

There is no such place as this in Scotland, but Ness is clearly coined from Loch Ness, the largest and most famous loch in Scotland. This loch flows into the River Ness which empties into the sea at Inverness (See Inver- above).

Glen Nevis

Inverness-shire

This whisky is named after a now-closed distillery in Campbeltown, although there is a glen with this name near **Ben Nevis**.

There was a style of Gaelic poetry that insulted various places, and one author had this to say about the glen:

> Gleann Nibheis, gleann nan clach
> Gleann 's am bi 'n gart anmoch,
> Gleann cumhang, gleann fàs,
> Gleann dubh fada fiadhaich grànd',
> 'S am beil sluagh a' mhì-ghnàthais,
> Gleann ris na chuir Dia a chùl,
> Amar-sgùrainn an domhain mhòir

> Glen Nevis, glen of the stones
> Glen wherein the corn is late,
> A narrow glen, an empty glen,
> A long black wild ugly glen,
> Where the abusive people are,
> A glen God has forsaken,
> The whole world's washing bowl

Glen Nicol

There is no such place as this in Scotland. It is 'whisky glen' (see p. 68) added to the personal name Nicol.

Glen Ord

Glen Ord Distillery relates to the place-name The Ord in the Black Isle, with the whisky glen- added on (see p. 68). The Ord (*Le Ord* in 1479) is in Gaelic called An t-Òrd, literally 'the hammer' [ən torsht] a fairly common Gaelic name, relating to the shape of the hill here. The nearby settlement **Muir of Ord** is known in Gaelic as Am Blàr Dubh 'the black moor'. See also **Glenordie**.

Glenordie

See **Glen Ord**, of which this is a variant.

Glen Orson

There is no such place as this. Could it commemorate the 1954 film *Trouble In the Glen*, starring Orson Welles?

Glen Parker

This is said to be from an 'unnamed' Speyside Distillery and no other information is available. There is no such place as Glen Parker and in all likelihood, it was coined from a surname, with the 'whisky glen' added (see p. 68) but this is just a guess.

Glen Quaich

Perthshire (*Glenqueith* in 1654) [glen kweec]

This is from Gaelic Gleann Cuaich 'Quaich glen' [g̊lauN ku-ic]. A quaich is a ceremonial bowl used in Scotland for drinking. The idea is that the river has quaich-shaped pools along it. Glen Quoich in Inverness-shire and in Braemar have the same underlying Gaelic form.

Glen Quaich has a reputation for being cold, and a Gaelic proverb about it ran: *Foghar Ghlinn Cuaich: gaoth a tuath is cruaidh-reòthadh* 'Autumn in Glen Quaich: a north wind and a hard frost'.

Glen Ranoch

There is no such place as this in Scotland, but the name is most likely the 'whisky glen' (see p. 68) added to the place-name Rannoch, which is spelled however with two n's. This is a region of Perthshire which is called Raineach in Gaelic, meaning 'bracken' [rañox].

Glenrosa

(*Glenrosse* in 1440)

This is Norse river-name in origin, from *Hrossá*, 'horse-river'. This was adopted as Rosa in Gaelic, and the glen through which it ran was then called Gleann Rosa [g̃lauN rosə] in Gaelic and subsequently Glen Rosa in English.

Glen Rossie

This name comprises the 'whisky glen' (see p. 68) with the place-name Rossie. There is more than one place with this name in Scotland, with more than one derivation. Some derive from Gaelic *ros,* which can mean either 'woods' or 'promontory' sometimes with the Gaelic suffix -aidh, thus Rosaidh either 'wooded place' or 'promontory place' [rosi]. There is, however, an island called Rosaidh that is actually from Norse *Hrosøy* 'horse island'. Dalarossie, however, is another excellent example of how place-names can be misleading. This is not a combination of Gaelic *dail* 'waterside meadow' and Rosaidh. The stress in the name is on the second syllable and the name is Gaelic Dail Fheargusa 'the haugh of Fergus'.

In more modern times, the brand was bought and promoted by Francis Rossi of Status Quo, presumably because of the similarity of the names.

Glenrothes

Moray (*Rothes* in 1337) [<u>roth</u>əz]

Glenrothes Distillery sits within the town of Rothes, which is in Gaelic Rathais [rahish] which might mean 'fortunate or lucky station' or, more likely, 'place of forts' from an old Gaelic word rath 'fort' [raa]. For the name of the distillery, the 'whisky glen' (see p. 68) has been added.

Confusingly, there is an actual settlement called Glenrothes in Fife, which was created in 1948, with a 'fake' Glen added to the name Rothes, commemorating the Earls of Rothes who owned part of the land occupied by the town.

Glen Rowan

There is no such place as this in Scotland. It seems to simply be the 'whisky glen' (see p. 68) with Rowan added on. Rowan is a girl's name or a type of tree.

Glen Rowland

There is no such place as this in Scotland. The name is comprised by the 'whisky glen' (see p. 68) and the name Rowland. This whisky was bottled in Glasgow for R. H. Macy & Co, an American company better known as Macy's, which was founded by the eponymous Rowland Hussy Macy (1822–77), so it would seem the whisky is named after him.

Glenroy, House of-

Lochaber (*Glenroy* in 1574)

Whilst there is a Glen Roy in Lochaber, the company known as House of Glenroy does not seem to have any connection it. Glen Roy is from Gaelic Gleann Ruaidh 'the glen of the River Ruaidh or Roy' [gĺauN rui]. Ruaidh is a river-name meaning 'red one', and is relates to Gaelic *ruadh* 'red' [ruəgh].

Glen Russell

There is no such place as this in Scotland. It seems to simply be the 'whisky glen' (see p. 68) with Russell added on. Russell is a man's name and a surname.

Glen Salen

Whilst there is no such place as Glen Salen in Scotland, there are two Salens in Scotland, one in Ardnamurchan and one on Mull. These are known in Gaelic as An t-Sàilean 'the inlet or arm of sea' [ən taalan]. The longer form for the one on the Isle of Mull was Sàilean Dubh

Chaluim Chille 'black Salen of Columba', whilst the Ardnamurchan example was known as Sàilean Loch Suaineart 'Salen of Loch Sunart'. Which one of these, if any, Glen Salen denotes, is unknown.

Glen Sannox

Arran (*Glensennock* in 1654)

This glen runs into the sea at a settlement called Sannox, after which the glen is obviously named. In Gaelic, it is Gleann Sannaig (glauN senik) and Sannox is Sannag (senak). The final -x is actually an English/Scots plural, as there were two settlements with this name nearby. The name Sannag is of Old Norse origin, from *Sandavík* 'sand bay', which has the same source as the word 'sandwich', from the Earl of Sandwich.

Glen Saunders

There is no such place as Glen Saunders. The name appears to be a variant of Saunders Blended Scotch Whisky which was bottled and blended by James Saunders & Co, Glasgow, a now-defunct whisky company.

Glen Scanlan

There is no such place as this in Scotland. It is the 'whisky glen' (see p. 68) added to the surname Scanlan. An earlier whisky by the same company was called Golden Scanlan.

Glenscoma

There is no such place as this, SCOMA GmbH is a German malt whisky bottling company.

Glen Scotia

This is an entirely fabricated name, using the Glen- element with the Latin name for Scotland: Scotia, as seen in the Canadian name Nova Scotia or 'new Scotland'.

This distillery takes its water from a reservoir called Crosshill Loch, named after the nearby farm. This is most likely a transparent name 'cross hill', perhaps a site of a cross at which people genuflected as they approach the chapel of Kilkerran.

Glen Shee

Perthshire (*glensche* in 1463)

This is from Gaelic: Gleann Sìth 'fairy glen' [glauN shịi]. *Sìth* is anglicised as shee in English, and the word Banshee comes from Gaelic *ban-sìth* 'fairy woman'. This glen is mentioned in a Gaelic poem from around 1500 (as such the Gaelic spelling below is archaic):

> Gleann Síodh an gleann so rém thaoibh
> i mbinn faoidh éan agus lon;
> minic rithidís an Fhéin
> ar an t-srath so an déidh a gcon.

> This glen beside me is Glen Shee,
> where blackbirds and other birds sing sweetly;
> often would the Fian run
> along this glen behind their hounds.

Glen Shira

Perthshire (*Glen Shyr* in c. 1591)

This name is from Gaelic Gleann Sìora [glauN shiira]. The meaning of Sìora is unknown but there is a Gaelic word *sìor* 'lasting', and it most likely relates to that, although its exact implication here is not clear.

Glenskiach

Ross and Cromarty

This distillery is in Evanton on a river called Abhainn Sgitheach [aviñ ski-ox] in Gaelic. *Abhainn* means river, whilst Skiach is an anglicised form of Sgitheach, which means 'hawthorn'. Thus, Abhainn Sgitheach means 'hawthorn river'. Again, the Glen part is constructed, as the river does not flow through Glen Skiach but Srath Sgitheach (*Scraiskeith* in 1479) [srah ski-ox]. See p. 148.

The actual site of the Glenskiach Distillery, before it was built in 1896, was known as Muileann an Fhuarain 'the mill of the spring' [mulǝN ǝn uarin].

Glen Sloy

Argyll [*Lochẽ[n] Sloy* in c. 1591)

Although there is no such place as Glen Sloy in Scotland, there is a well-known body of water called Loch Sloy. In Gaelic, this is Loch Sluaigh [lox slui], although a variant form was Lochan Sluaigh [loxan slui]. Here *lochan* means 'little loch' which is an odd name as it is of considerable size. *Sluaigh* in Gaelic means 'people, folk' but can also relate to the fairy folk, and this may be the meaning here.

Glen Spey

This relates to the River Spey, with the added 'Glen'. For a discussion of the name Spey, see **Speyside**.

The water source for this distillery in Rothes is said to be Donnie Burn, but it is called simply 'the Burn of Rothes' on maps. This burn nonetheless flows past two hills called Muckle (large) and Little Dounie, and it is perhaps from these that Donnie Burn took its name. Dounie is likely from Dùnaidh 'fort-place' from Gaelic *dùn*, see p. 56.

The Glen Stag

There is no such place-name in Scotland. It seems to take its name from the 'whisky glen' (see p. 68) with Stag added. The cover of the bottle is reminiscent of the Monarch of the Glen, a famous Scottish painting of a stag.

Glen Storn

There is no such place as this in Scotland. It is the 'whisky glen' (see p. 68) added to the word Storn, which does not mean anything in any language of Scotland. This whisky was, however, bottled for the German audience, and Storn is a surname in that country, so it perhaps relates to that.

Glen Talloch

There is no such place-name as this in Scotland. It may come from the place-name Poltalloch in Argyle with Pol swapped for the 'whisky glen' (see p. 68). Pol- is from Gaelic *poll* 'pool'.

The word Scot is, of course, used for the people of Scotland today, but originally it was applied to the people we now call the Irish, as the *Scotti.*

The Gaelic word for Scotland is Alba (earlier Albainn), and this usage is the remnant of an old word for the whole of Britain, which is still used poetically sometimes as Albion; in Welsh the word is *Elbid.* This term was originally used to describe the whole world, and then just Britain, and finally Scotland. The derivation of the word is not clear, but it may be cognate with Latin *albus* 'white' and be supposed to denote the 'light world' above ground as opposed to the dark underworld. Whatever the original meaning, it also appears in other region names, such as Albany and Albania in other languages.

Glen Tarras

Dumfries and Galloway

This is coined from the Tarras Water, and although there is no Glen Tarras, such a name would be topographically appropriate. Tarras is an ancient river-name, likely from a root *$t\bar{a}$- 'melting, flowing' from which the name of the River Tay may also derive. The sections of the Tarras can be dangerous, which led to the Scots saying:

> Was ne'er ane drownied in Tarras,
> Nor yet in doubt,
> For ere the head wins down,
> The harns are out.

Loosely translated this means: Nobody was ever drowned in the Tarras, or in danger of being so, because before their head was submerged, their brains were dashed on the rocks.

Glentauchers

The name Glentauchers did not exist before the distillery was built, but records show two small settlements were once here, one called Tauchers or Tachars and the other Mill of Tauchers. The former is now the site of the distillery. Current maps also show a Burn of Tauchers near the site of Glentauchers Distillery. *Taucher* or *tocher* is a Scots word for a 'dowry', more likely however the name comes from Gaelic *tochar* 'causeway' [toxər], denoting a way across the river here.

Glen Torness

There is no such place as Glen Torness in Scotland, but there are a number of places simply called Torness. In the Highlands, the names derive from Tòrr an Eas 'the hill of the waterfall' [toor ən es]. One in East Lothian near Edinburgh, however, is more likely from Old Scots *torr ness* 'rocky promontory' which describes it perfectly.

Glen Torran

Whilst there is no such place as this in Scotland, there are several places called Torran and it is not clear which place is meant. These names can come from one of two distinct but related Gaelic place-names, both related to Gaelic *tòrr* 'hill'. One is An Torran 'the little hill' [ən toRan], and the other is Na Torran 'the hills' [nə toRən]. The suffix -an in Gaelic can denote a plural or a diminutive.

Glentoshan

There is no such place as Glentoshan, rather, this is a brand of **Auchentoshan**. Thus, it seems Auchen- has been swapped for Glen- in this instance.

Glen Tress

Scottish Borders (*Glentress* in 1654)

This glen near Peebles in the Borders is either Gaelic or British in origin. If Gaelic it would represent what would be written in modern orthography as Gleann Treas 'battle glen', while if British in origin the name would be Glinn Tres meaning the same thing. The *tress* word, besides meaning 'battle', can mean 'violence', and it may be that this was originally applied to the river here, meaning 'violently flowing river'.

Glentromie

Inverness-shire (*Glen-Trummie* in c. 1591) [glen <u>trou</u>mi]

Glentromie is a Gaelic name in origin, from Gleann Tromaidh [g̃lauN tromi]. Gleann is 'glen' and Tromaidh is the name of the river here, which is likely connected with the Gaelic word *trom* 'heavy', meaning 'the heavy one', perhaps relating to the flow of the water in some way.

Glen Turner

This is not a place-name. No other information is forthcoming, but the Glen is the 'whisky glen' (see p. 68) whilst Turner most likely relates to a personal name.

Glenturret

Perthshire (*aquam de Turret* in 1572)

Glen Turret is named after the river called the Burn of Turret. The name in Gaelic is Turraid or perhaps Turaid, itself from an earlier Celtic root which is seen in Gaelic as *tur* 'dry', the idea being that it is a river which dries up in the summer.

Glen Tyrell

This is not a place-name but the name of a blend. Tyrell is a surname of Irish origin and most likely the name comes from that surname somehow.

Glenugie

Aberdeenshire

The River Ugie flows through Buchan and enters the sea near Peterhead, but rises as two separate watercourses, now known as the North Ugie Water and the South Ugie Water, before merging into the River Ugie. Nowadays, the two waters are denoted by their geographical relation to each other; in the fifteenth century however, they were known in Scots as the Back Ugie and Fore Ugie, respectively.

Previously, the River Ugie appeared around AD 1150 in the Book of Deer – one of the earliest examples of Scottish Gaelic. There the South

Ugie Water is mentioned as *dubuci,* which in modern Gaelic would be *Dubh Uige,* that is, the *dubh* or 'black' Ugie. The North Ugie Water is not mentioned but possibly this was the *find* (modern Gaelic *fionn*) or 'White' Ugie. The name *Uige* itself is likely of pre-Gaelic origin and its original meaning is not known. There is no such place as Glen Ugie in Scotland however (though there is one in Australia).

Glenury Royal

Angus

Glenury comes from Ury, a place near Stonehaven. It possibly comes from a Gaelic word *iùbhrach* 'yew tree', thus An Iùbhraidh 'the yew tree area'. It is perhaps interesting that one writer, when visiting the Ury estate in 1867 remarked: 'Numerous beeches of startling dimensions grace the lawn, and near where stood the old homestead a yew tree now in the strength of its power, reminds one that it might have enjoyed, probably did enjoy, youth contemporaneously with the ancient Laird of Ury'.

Glen Usk

This is a blended Scotch whisky which was bottled for the Glen Usk Whisky company based in Brecon, Wales. The River Usk flows past Brecon, thus the name is a combination of the 'whisky glen' (see p. 68) and the Welsh River Usk. The Usk comes from Welsh Wysg, an old word that may have originally simply meant 'water'. This and other similar sound river-names in the British Isles such as the Esk, The Exe and the Axe are all thought to be related. See **Glenesk**.

Glenvar

Although there is a Glenvar in Donegal, Ireland, most likely this name was simply invented as a Scottish-sounding place-name for Italian audiences for whom this whisky bottling was made.

Glen Vegan

There is no such place-name as this in Skye, rather it appears to be based on the Skye place-name Dunvegan, with Glen- swapped for Dun-. See **Dun Bheagan** for discussion of Dunvegan.

GlenWyvis

There is no such place, strictly speaking, as Glen Wyvis, this has been taken from the name of the nearby mountain Ben Wyvis, with Glen swapped for Ben. (See **Ben Wyvis** for a discussion of that name).

The water from this distillery is taken from Dochcarty Burn; Dochcarty is a nearby settlement which comes from Gaelic Dabhach Gartaidh 'the davoch land of the corn enclosure' [dox garshti].

Grangestone

Ayrshire (*Grangetoun* in 1747–55)

Grangestone is a blend owned by William Grant & Sons, a company who owns Girvan Distillery, whose site is at a place called Grangeston in Ayrshire outside Girvan. Grangeston (without the e) appears to be from Scots *grange* 'granary' or 'farm' and *toun* 'farm, town'. The -e was added to the name when naming the whisky for some reason.

Great King Street

This is the name of a street in Edinburgh's New Town. It was originally called simply King Street, named, along with many other streets in the area, in 1802 to commemorate King George III. The 'Great' was added in 1812 to avoid confusion with another King Street elsewhere in Edinburgh.

Hazelburn

Kintyre, Argyll

This relates to a distillery in Campbeltown. *Burn* is the Scots word for 'stream' (see p. 159); there is, however, no record of a Hazel Burn running through Campbeltown, and it would seem this name has been invented. Two interesting points should be taken into account though:

The only stream or burn to run nearby is Witch Burn; this is known in Gaelic is Abhainn nam Buidseach 'the river of the witches' [aviñ nəm butshox]. It is possible that the marketers of this whisky wished to use the name Witchburn but chose to reinterpret it as witch-hazel, and thus as hazel.

At variants with the above point is that a very short way from the distillery is Calton Hill. Perhaps the word Calton is an anglicisation of the Gaelic word for 'hazel', which is *calltainn*.

Highland Esk

See **Glenesk**.

Highland Park

Orkney

The name of the most northerly distillery is said to be taken from a pre-existing name of a small farm called High Park or High Park of Rosebank; in Orkney Scots, a *park* can mean a 'field' or 'farm'. This explanation is found commonly but the author has been unable to find any contemporary evidence for this.

The Highlands is the term in Scotland broadly used to denote the northern mountainous area of mainland Scotland, literally 'the uplands'. This distillery is near Kirkwall, Orkney, which is only considered the Highlands within the definition of the whisky regions, where the Highlands reaches much further south and north than is generally understood. The whisky world defines Highland in a very different way than is generally accepted by geographers.

Hillhead

Orkney

There are several places called Hillhead on Orkney, and this one surely relates to the one just south of the Highland Park Distillery. The word *hill* in Orkney Scots, and in other dialects, can denote a strip of uncultivated land between a township and common moor.

Hillside

Angus

This is named after the relatively modern settlement of Hillside near Montrose, which was set up when a 'lunatic asylum' was established, as they were called then. There is no particularly notable hill in the area, so the name may have been transferred from elsewhere. Alternatively, *hill* in Scots can also mean 'a common moor or upland used for grazing'.

Hobbister

Orkney (*Howbuster* in 1492) [h̲o̲bəstər]

There are several places on Orkney with this name; this one relates to a site on the Mainland, which is the source of peat for the Highland Park Distillery. This is a Norse name from the elements *haugr* 'a mound' (see **Hoebeg** and **Ardnahoe**) and *bólstaðr* 'homestead'.

Hoebeg

The blurb on this whisky's box states 'Hoebeg is Gaelic for "*small rocky hill*" overlooking a safe harbour'. This seems to be a translation of Gaelic Hogha Beag. *Hogha* is a word of Norse derivation from *haugr* originally meaning 'burial cairn' with a later development into 'any rocky mound', whilst *beag* means 'small'. Although this is an Islay whisky, there is no such place as this on that island. There is such a place on North Uist with this name however (*Holebeg* in 1807), as well as a Howbeg on South Uist, with the same underlying Gaelic form.

Holyrood

Edinburgh (*Sancti Crucis* in 1128, a Latin form)

This well-known Edinburgh name is from Scots *haly* 'holy' and *rood* 'cross', denoting 'the church of the Holy Cross' relating to the Abby founded here by David I in 1128. Then it was referred to by a Latin translation of *Sancti Crucis*.

Hunter's Glen

There is no such place-name as this in Scotland; it would seem to be purely fabricated. It appears to be unrelated to Glen Hunter.

Huntly

Moray (*Huntleie* in 1165–82)

Aberdeenshire in Moray is transferred from a place in Berwickshire, whence the Earls of Huntly got their name. This name is Scots or Old English in origin, probably from *hund* 'dog' (i.e. hound) and *ley* 'clearing', thus 'dog clearing'. The Gordons brought this name with them to Moray in medieval times. The settlement was also called Strathbogie and even up until the 1950s it was known in Gaelic as Srath Bhalgaidh [srah valəki], the Gaelic form of the name. The name is now Hunndaidh [huuNdi] in Gaelic which derives from English Huntly.

Ila Insvla

This Islay bottling takes its name from the name of an early map of Islay dated to 1654 made by a Johann Blaeu in his Atlas Novus or 'New Atlas'. Insvla is Latin *insula* 'island'. See **Islay**.

Inchdairnie

Fife (*Inchdrayn* in 1332–50) [insh dairni]

This is a Gaelic name in origin, from something like Innis Droighne 'island or haugh of blackthorn' [iinsh droinə]. For *innis* or *inch*, see p. 109. *Droighne* is a form of *droigheann* meaning 'bramble or blackthorn'.

Inchfad

Stirlingshire (*Inchefad* in 1329)

This island is one of several in Loch Lomond; it comes from An Innis Fhad(a) 'the long island' [ən iinsh atə]. See also **Inchmoan**.

Inchgower

Moray [insh gauər]

Inchgower Inn appears on nineteenth-century maps near the site of the current Inchgower Distillery. The name Inchgower itself is presumably from a Gaelic Innis Gobhar 'goat island' [iinsh go-ər].

Innis / Inch

The Gaelic word *innis* is often translated as 'island', and in the east this is certainly true, as seen in the names of many of the islands in the Firth of forth such as Inchkeith. The name can also denote a raised patch of dry land in a swampy area and thus the element is seen in inland place-names as well, such as in the name Inchture near Dundee. In Wester Ross *innis* can denote a small mound on which cattle congregate to keep their feet dry.

Inchmoan

Argyll (*Ynismoin* in 1208–65)

This is Gaelic: Innis Mòine, meaning 'peat or moss Island' [iinsh moñə]. The inhabitants of Luss nearby used to obtain fuel in the form of peat from this island. In a list of Gaelic meanings for the islands of Loch Lomond from 1701, the name is described as 'Inch moin or the Mosse or peat isle'. The whisky itself is in fact peaty although the distillery is not physically on the island, nor does it use peat from this island.

Inchmurrin

Dunbartonshire (*elan rosduue* c. 1224–34 and *Inchemuryn* 1393)

This is the name of an island in Loch Lomond. In Gaelic, it is called Innis Mearain 'the island of Saint Mearan' [iinsh merin]. Very little is known about this saint, even if it was a man or woman. The island was also known as Eilean an Rois Dhuibhe, meaning in Gaelic 'the island of Rossdhu' [elan ən ros ghuuyə]; Rossdhu is a peninsula on the shore of Loch Lomond and was originally in Gaelic An Ros Dubh 'the black peninsula' [ən ros duu].

Inveralmond

Perthshire (*Rathinueramon* in 862)

This name is Gaelic: Inbhir Amain 'the foot of (the river) Almond or Aman' [iñər amin], where Almond or Aman derives from a pre-Gaelic root. The spelling of the word Almond is modern and has nothing to do with the type of nut. A Pictish king called Domnal mac Ailpín died in a place called *Rathinueramon* in 862; this is in modern Gaelic Ràth Inbhir Amain 'the fort of Inveralmond', a site just north of Perth.

Inverarity

Angus (*Inuerarecthin* in 1173–78)

Inver is from Gaelic *inbhir* 'inlet, confluence' (see p. 1). The second element always denotes a watercourse. In this case, there is a small unnamed burn here which flows into the Kerbet Water, this was presumably once called the Arity. This name may reflect Aradaidh [arəti] in Gaelic, which itself possibly comes from a Brittonic root, akin to the modern Welsh word *araf* 'slow', thus the river would have originally meant 'the slow running one'.

Inveravon

Banff (*Inuerouen* in 1187–1203)

There are several places in Scotland with this name, but this is a Speyside Malt, and therefore must relate to the River Avon, a tributary of the Spey. This name means 'the inlet of the River Avon'. For the element Inver, see p. 1; for the name of the Avon, see **Bridge of Avon**.

Inverdice

There is no such place-name as this in Scotland. It appears to be Inver (see p. 1) with the word -dice at the end. Possibly the name Allardice has been used here as an analogy. Allardice is both a village in Kincardineshire and a common surname.

Invergordon

Ross and Cromarty

Although Invergordon is a real place, the place-name is not a 'real' Inver- name as such; it was coined in 1760 after the former proprietor Sir Alex Gordon, with the Inver- added to give it an air of authenticity (see p. 1). It is naturally referred to nowadays in Gaelic as Inbhir Ghòrdain using the same elements as if it means 'the inlet of the *River

Gordon', although there is no such watercourse. Before the founding of Invergordon however, the place was referred to in Gaelic either simply as An Rubha 'the promontory' [ən ruə] or as the longer name of Rubha Aonach Breacaidh 'the point of Breakie market' [ruə wnox brexkox]. Breacaidh or Breakie was the name of a stream here.

Inver House

In 1936 Mr Simon Neuman (head of Publicker Industries from 1933–76) bought a mansion called Laurento in Wayne, Philadephia, America. He renamed it Inver House, and later gave the same name to a whisky called Inver House Rare. When Publicker Industries expanded, they bought some land in Airdrie on which to build a distillery and named it Inver House Distillers. The original house in Philadelphia has since been pulled down and a street called Inveraray now runs where the house once was. Why it was originally called Inver House is not known, but given that Mr Neuman expanded into Scotland in the 1950s, he may have had an interest in Scotland from before that time, and decided to give his house a Scottish-sounding name. See also **Glen Flagler**, where Neuman called a whisky after another place where he lived.

Islay

(*in Ilea insula* in c. 700 in Latin)

Islay is immediately from Gaelic *Ìle* [iìlə]. The English spelling with an -s- is non-historical and has come about purely through an analogy with the words 'isle' and 'island'. As mentioned in the introduction, the names of many of the larger islands are very ancient, and their language of origin and original meanings are often obscure. Several viable suggestions have been made for the derivation of *Ìle*, but we cannot be certain about any of them.

Islay mu Dheas

This sort of means 'South Islay'; *mu dheas* [mu yes] is one way of denoting 'South' in Gaelic. The correct Gaelic form would be Ìle mu Dheas. See **Islay** above.

Islebrae

If we take this name at face value, the name would be Scots *isle* 'island' and *brae* 'hillslope', but there is no evidence that a place called Islebrae ever existed. Thus, it appears to be a twentieth-century name for the whisky only. Braefoot is near Killyloch Distillery, where this whisky was made, and there are several other Brae- names nearby as well. Spiers Island is on Hillend Reservoir which was built 1797–99. It is thus possible the name is a portmanteau of these two places.

Isle of Harris

Western Isles (*na Hearadh* in c. 1500)

This is a name of Norse origin, from *Herað* '(the) district'. Many of the larger islands in the Western Isles derive from Norse. In Gaelic, it is Na Hearadh [nə herəgh]; words in Gaelic do not normally start with an H- and in order to be able to reproduce the sound naturally, the plural article was added to fit Gaelic phonology. Thus, in origin the name is not a plural. Harris itself is not strictly speaking an island, rather it comprises part of a large island, the other greater part of which is Lewis.

Isle of Jura

Hebrides (*insule de Dure* in 1336)

The name Jura originates from Norse *Dýrøy* 'deer island'; this is an apt name, as to this day there are far more deer than people on the island. It then became Gaelic Diùra [juura] and thence English Jura.

The name of the distillery was known in Gaelic as An Teanga 'the tongue' [ən tchengə], generally denoting a tongue-shaped piece of land, sometimes between two burns. The source of the water for the distillery comes ultimately from Loch a' Bhaile-Mhargaidh 'the loch of the market town' [lox ə valə varəki], an odd name, since the loch is in a remote upland region most unsuited for commerce.

Isle of Raasay

See **Raasay**.

Jericho
Aberdeenshire

This is coined from a place in Aberdeenshire called Jericho, or rather, Nether Jericho (*nether* is the Scots word for 'lower'). This is, of course, coined from the place referred to in the Old Testament. It is notable that the burn which runs here is also called the Jordan. The habit of transferring names from places mentioned in the Bible to Scotland was a common fashion in the eighteenth and nineteenth centuries. There are several Jerichos, Jordans, Joppas and Egypts, for example.

Jura, Isle of-
See **Isle of Jura**.

The Kenmore

There are several places with this name in Scotland and they come from Gaelic A' Cheannmhor 'the big head' [ə cauNəvor]. They are usually at the end of a loch; the best-known example is the one at the end of Loch Tay. It is interesting that the Gaelic form of the name and the name of this whisky has a definite article ('the'), but the English form of the place-name does not have the article. It is also noteworthy that the Gaelic forms are feminine in gender, whilst *ceann* 'head' is masculine in normal speech.

Kilbride Dam
Islay (*Kilbreid* in 1541)

This is named after the body of water (marked simply as 'reservoir' on modern maps) which is the source of water for the **Laphraoig** Distillery. It is named after nearby Kilbride, or Cille Bhrìghde [kìlə vriijə] as it is known in Gaelic, which means 'the church of St Bridget'. The remains of her chapel are still visible on the farmlands today. This is a common name, especially in Argyll, and St Bridget probably lived in Kildare, Ireland around the sixth century AD.

CILL 'CHURCH'

Cill (or *cille* as it is sometimes pronounced) is a word no longer used in Gaelic, but still appears in place-names to denote a church, and is nearly always followed by the name of a saint. It was borrowed from Latin *cella* 'monk's cell' a word which also gives us the English word *cell*, in the sense of a monk's cell. The term is anglicised as Kil-, in names such as Kilbride and Kilchoman.

Kilchoman

Islay (*Kilcoman* in 1507) [kilxomən]

Kilchoman is Gaelic in origin, from Cill Chomain [kiiᶅ xomin]. It is often very difficult to identify which saint is commemorated in which place-name, or even if any given saint existed at all. In all likelihood though, Coman or Commán was a saint who lived in the eighth century and was associated with Roscommon in Ireland.

The water source for this distillery has a Gaelic name: Allt Gleann Osamail, meaning 'the burn of Glen Osamail'. The last word here is ultimately from a Norse *Óssholmr* 'inlet holm'.

Kildalton

See **Crois Chill Daltain**.

Kildonan

Arran (*Kildonen* in 1609) [kildonən]

There are several places in Scotland with this name, and this one relates to the place on Arran. For Kil-, see above. This name is from Gaelic Cill Donnain 'St Donnan's church' [kiiᶅ doNin]. Donnan was a popular saint who was martyred on the Isle of Eigg in 617.

Kilkerran

Kintyre, Argyll (*Kilchiarane* in 1210) [kilkerən]

Kilkerran is from Gaelic Cille Chiarain, meaning 'the church of Ciarán' [kiȋlə ciərin]; it is now part of modern Campbeltown. Saint Ciarán is generally taken to be Ciarán of Cluain Mac Nois, who died in 549. He appears several times in place-names; there are other instances of Cille Chiarain on Lismore and Islay, for example.

See **Campbeltown Loch** for further discussion.

Killyloch

Lanarkshire

It is said that this name is from a misprint on bottles of the name of the nearby Lilly Loch. It is not clear if this is true or not; it may be that the name Lillyloch was changed to Killyloch to make it sound more Gaelic, as if the name began with the common Kil- (see p. 114). The name Lilly Loch, of course, means 'a loch (or lake) filled with lillies'.

Kilmartin Glen

Argyll (*Kilmartyne* in 1547) [kil<u>martin</u>]

Kilmartin Glen in Argyll is a glen which contains the settlement of Kilmartin. This is from Gaelic Cill Mhàrtainn meaning 'the church of St Martin' [kiȋl vaarshtchin]. St Martin of Tours was a popular saint in Scotland, and he appears many times in Scottish place-names. There is a Gaelic poem written in praise of Kilmartin Glen, which begins thus:

Gleann Chille Mhàrtainn far an d'fhuair mi m'àrach,
'S e an gleann is àillidh leam tha fon ghrèin,
Le thulaich neòinein 's le shliosaibh bòidheach,
'S a shraithean chòmhnard tha math gu feum.

Kilmartin Glen where I was raised
To me it is the most beautiful under the Sun
With its hills of daisies and with beautiful slopes
And its level straths that are good to use.

Kincaple

Fife (*Kinecapel* in 1212)

This is a name of Gaelic origin, ostensibly from Ceann Capall 'head of a work-horse'. Gaelic has not been spoken in Fife for hundreds of years however, so what exactly this was supposed to mean as a place-name is unclear. Most likely it was meant to denote the 'end or head of land called Capall', where perhaps Capall was a place named after the horse in a pre-Christian totemic sense, or was simply a place which specialised in horse-rearing.

Kinclaith

Glasgow (*Conclut* in 862) [kincl<u>ai</u>th]

Kinclaith is a lost name denoting the area now known as Glasgow Green, a piece of land in the centre of Glasgow. This name shows British influence but may have Gaelic elements. Con- or Kin- was likely from *con 'with, together'. The -*claith* or -*clud* portion of the name probably refers to the name of the River Clyde. Thus, the name likely meant 'the confluence of the Clyde' (with the Molendinar Burn).

Kingsbarns

Fife (*Northbarnis* in 1329)

This Fife place-name is transparent: 'the King's barns' although it has an earlier name *Northbarnis* in 1329 which would be 'Northbarns' today. St Andrews has several local royal associations, see under that name for more details.

Kininvie

Moray (*Kynninveir* in 1579) [ki<u>nin</u>vi]

Kininvie is perhaps from Gaelic Ceann Fhinn-Mhuighe 'end of the white plain' [kyauN iin vooyə].

Kinloch

Kintyre, Argyll

Kinloch is another name for Campbeltown (or at least is a part of it); it comes from Gaelic Ceann Locha 'the end of the loch' [kyauN loxə], which perfectly describes the site. There are street names to this day containing the name. It is no coincidence that the place is right next to Lochend, which is a Scots version of the name. See also **Kilkerran** and **Campbeltown Loch**.

Kirkland

'Kirkland Signature' is a brand owned and created by Costco, a multinational chain of retail stores. Its former headquarters were in Kirkland, a city in Washington, America, which was named in the 1880s after its founder, British-born steel tycoon Peter Kirk.

Kirkwall Bay

Orkney (*Kirkiovagi* in c. 1102)

Kirkwall in Orkney is an excellent example of how place-names can be deceptive. The name appears to be Scots *kirk* 'church' and *wall*. The name, as the early form above shows, is actually Norse, from *Kirkjuvágr* 'church bay'. The final -*ll* comes from a reanalysis; Scots often drops the final -ll in words, such as *ba'* for 'ball' or *wa'* for 'wall'. The name in Scots sounds like Kirkwa, which people seem to have 'corrected' into Kirkwall, though the final -ll has no historical authenticity.

Knockando

Moray (*Knock Andich* in c. 1591) [nokandou]

The text on a bottle of Knockando claims that this name means in Gaelic 'the black little hill', presumably as if *An Cnocan Dubh, although often glossed ungrammatically as 'Cnoc-an-Dubh'. This would be a reasonable assumption if one were looking at the name in text only. In fact, the real Gaelic form is quite different, being Cnoc Cheannachd 'the hill of buying' [kroxk cauNoxk]. The early spelling also supports this. Presumably the hill was the site of a market of some sort, but this has been lost to history.

The water that serves this distillery is from a spring at Cardnach, a small nearby farm. Cardnach may be from a Pictish or early Gaelic element *carden* meaning 'enclosure'. It no longer exists in the modern language, except in place-names, such as Kincardine and **Pluscarden**.

Knockdhu and anCnoc

Moray

The original place here was the big hill known in Gaelic as An Cnoc meaning 'the hill' and in locally in Scots as the Knock, where *knock* is a Scots word for 'hill', derived from the Gaelic word. This hill then gave its name to the nearby settlement of Knock. When the whisky was named, it was for some reason called Knockdhu, as if from Cnoc Dubh 'black hill' (see p. 30 for the spelling of -dhu). There is, however, no record that the hill was ever known as anything other than simply An Cnoc or The Knock.

This whisky was renamed as anCnoc in 1994 as it sounded too much like the name of the nearby whisky distillery Knockando. AnCnoc is a good stab at the Gaelic orthography, though it would be better spelled as two words 'An Cnoc'. It is pronounced in Gaelic as [ən krohk], despite what is written on the bottle itself (*a*-nock).

Ladyburn

Ayrshire

There is no Lady Burn on the maps, but there was once a small settlement called Ladywell nearby Girvan Distillery, which now gives its name to Ladywell Avenue which runs through the distillery. Ladywell is a common place-name, denoting a well or spring dedicated to the Virgin Mary, commonly referred to as 'Our Lady'. Ladywell was likely changed to Ladyburn, where *burn* is Scots for 'stream', see p. 159.

Lagavulin

Islay (*Lagavuline* in 1801) [lakəvulin]

This Islay name is Gaelic in origin, from Lag a' Mhuilinn 'the hollow of the mill' [lakəvuliñ]. Mills appear often in whisky names, because the same things are needed in the production of whisky as of flour: a flow of water. The Lagavulin Distillery sits on a river called Abhainn nam Beitheachan, Gaelic for 'the river of the beasts' [aviñ nəm behaxən].

In 1901 a Gael wrote about this place:

Thug Ìleach turas uaireigin gu Lag a' Mhuilinn, far an d'fhuair e cus ri òl. Seo mar a thuirt e:
'Lag a' Mhuilinn, lag mo dhunach, lag bu duilich fhàgail'.

An Islay man once took a trip to Lagavulin, where he had too much to drink. This is what he said:
'Lagavulin [i.e. the hollow of the mill], hollow of my misfortune, a hollow I would be sorry to leave'.

Lagg

Arran (*Lagg of Torrelin* in 1718)

This Arran name is from Gaelic An Lag 'the hollow' [ən lak]. This is a common element on Arran and elsewhere.

Laphroaig

Islay (*Laphroaig* in 1792) [lafro̲-ik]

This place-name defies formal explanation but it is almost certainly Norse in origin, having passed into Gaelic and now English. It may have been simply Old Norse *Breiðavík* 'broad bay' (in reference to Loch Laphroaig) which then evolved into Gaelic Proaig (there is a different place called Proaig to the north end of Islay, and this was spelled *Broag* in 1507). The development from this Norse form into the Gaelic form would be an odd development however, so another element other than *breið* 'broad' may have been present in the original name.

This name then perhaps gave rise to Lag Phroaig meaning 'the hollow of Proaig'. The problem with this derivation is that they would not yield Laphroaig in modern Gaelic. It may be that the name has undergone folk-etymology as if it were Latha Phroaig 'the day or battle of Proaig'. Proaig is known in local history as being the place where several hundred MacDonalds were killed in battle after the Battle of Tràigh Ghruinneart in 1598. Although Laphroaig is not particularly close to Proaig or the site of the battle, the battle was an important enough event that the name of Laphroaig was altered. Indeed the name is spelled in Gaelic sometimes in this format as if meaning 'the day (in the sense of battle) of Praoig'.

This whisky name is somewhat notorious as being 'unpronounceable'. A completely different whisky is called Laughfrog as a joke reference to this name.

Largiemeanoch

Arran (*Largymenoch* in 1766) [larg<u>imeno</u>x]

This Arran place-name is spelled Largymeanoch on maps now. There are three places with the name Largy on Arran: Largymeanoch from Gaelic Leargaidh Mheadhanach 'middle Largy' [leraki ve-anox]; Largybeg from Gaelic Leargaidh Bheag 'small Largy' [l<u>e</u>rəki vek] and Largymore from Gaelic Leargaidh Mhòr 'big Largy' [l<u>e</u>rəki voor]. Leargaidh itself means 'sloping place'.

Ledaig

Isle of Mull [l<u>e</u>dik]

This name occurs several times in the Highlands and reflects the Gaelic form An Leideag. The meaning of this is unclear but possibly comes from *leathaideag*, 'small slope' [le-atik], a diminutive form of *leathad* 'slope' [le-at].

The Lincluden

Dumfries and Galloway (*Lincloudan* in 1425) [linkl<u>u</u>dən]

Lincluden (without the definite article) is the name of Pictish or British origin which contains two elements. The first syllable is from *lann* 'open land'. The rest denotes the existing name Cluden, which is an old river-name from the same root as the name of the Clyde, but with a suffix -an. (See **Strathclyde** for a discussion of Clyde). Lincluden does in fact sit on the banks of the River Cluden.

Lindores Abbey

Fife (*Lundors* in 1178–82) [lin<u>do</u>rz]

Lindores is probably a Gaelic name, possibly from *lann*, an old word for a 'church' and *doras* 'door' in the sense of a 'pass' through a landscape, thus 'church at the pass'. The ruins of the abbey (founded c. 1190) sit directly opposite the site of the modern distillery.

Nicknames

It is common in traditional Gaelic culture to give nicknames to people who live in a particular township. The following is a stanza containing nicknames of people who lived in villages which had whisky distilleries on Islay:

Geàrr-ghobagan na h-Àirde Bige,
Cearcan dàite Lag a' Mhuilinn,
Tunnagan Laphroaig,
Balaich thapaidh Phort Eilidh,
Is cuthagan na h-Obha.

The short dog fish of Ardbeg
The scorched hens of Lagavulin
The ducks of Laphroaig
The clever boys of Port Ellen
And the cuckoos of the Oa.

Lingdarroch

Dumfries and Galloway [ling darox]

This bottling is made by **Bladnoch** Distillery, and it is surely no coincidence then that Lingdarroch is the name of a small pool on the River Bladnoch. Although in the south of Scotland, Gaelic was once spoken here, and has left many place-names behind. Lingdarroch is from Gaelic An Linne Dharach 'the oak-tree pool' [ən liñə gharox].

A Scots poem about Bladnoch and this pool (spelled Lindarroch) from 1888 goes:

I met my Maid by Bladnoch side
Lindarroch's woods were clothed in green
And sweetly smiled the sylvan scene
All Nature wore her Summer pride
That calm still eve by Bladnoch side.

Linkwood

Moray (*Linkwood* in c. 1591)

Whilst this is certainly a name of Scots origin, the meaning of 'link' is not exactly clear. A *link* can mean a chain or a bend, alternatively, *links* in the plural can denote 'a grassy area near the sea', such as with Leith Links in Edinburgh. *Wood* is as it seems.

The water for this distillery comes from Milbuies Loch. Milbuies is likely from either Gaelic *maol* [mwl] or *meall* [myauL] both meaning 'hill' with *buidhe* 'yellow' [buyə].

Linlithgow

West Lothian (*Linlidcu* in 1138) [linlithgou]

Linlithgow is a fascinating name with a history involving many of Scotland's languages. The name Linlithgow is of 'British' origin. In all likelihood, the name originally meant 'the pool of the damp or grey hollow', relating to what is now Linlithgow Loch. The modern Gaelic form of the name, Gleann Iucha, may seem utterly different from this but is probably the result of a Gaelic reinterpretation of this name into *Gleann Fhliuch Chu meaning 'glen of (the) wet hollow' [ğlauN lyiux xu] which was changed in natural speech to Gleann Iucha. (The fh- is silent in Gaelic).

Moreover, the name was reinterpreted again by Gaelic speakers as *Linn Liath Chu, 'pool of the grey dog' [liñ lia xuu]. A memory of this version of the name can be seen locally in the burgh crest which depicts a black dog, whilst locals call themselves 'Black Bitches'. The name is locally shortened to Lithgae [lithgi] in Scots.

See also the Wonders of Scotland on p. 136.

Little Bay

This is a type of Oban malt, and 'little bay' is simply a translation from Gaelic into English of this name. See **Oban**.

Littlemill

Dunbartonshire

This name is as it sounds, a Scots name from *little* and *mill*. Mills and distilleries both use running water to function, so it is no surprise that they sometimes use the same site.

Lochan Sholum / Lochan Solan

Islay [loxan holəm / loxan solən]

Lochan Sholum is a small loch on Islay which appears to be the source of Abhainn nam Beitheachan, the river that supplies **Lagavulin** Distillery. Lochan Sholum means 'the small loch of Solum', where Solum (now spelled Solam) is the name of a tiny nearby settlement. This is a name of Norse derivation, probably from *Sólheimr*, 'sunny place'. A number of other places with this name exist in Scotland and Scandinavia.

Loch

Loch was originally a Gaelic word to denote a body of water larger than a pool but smaller than a sea. It can denote either an inland lake or a sea-loch or inlet which are common in the western mainland. The word was borrowed into Scots, pronounced just the same, as *loch*. In all likelihood, the Pictish language also had the word, perhaps pronounced as *luch*. English *lake* is cognate with this word, coming from the same Indo-European root **lokus* into Latin *lacus*, then French *lac* and finally into English *lake*.

(Royal) Lochnagar

Aberdeenshire (*L. Garr* in 1654) [loxnəgar]

The name of this famous mountain contains is a puzzle: why does this mountain have the name of a loch? The exact reason is unknown but the name itself comes from a small loch on the north face of the mountain, called *Loch na Gàire*, 'the loch of the outcry' [lox nə gairə], thought to take its name from the howling of the wind among the rocks.

This gives rise to the question, what was the mountain originally called in Gaelic? The answer is *Beinn nan Cìochan*, 'the hill of the paps' [biñ nə kiixən] (*pap* is used here in the sense of 'hill'). This was the name recorded from the last generation of native speakers of Aberdeenshire Gaelic. The paps in question are called in Scots the

Meikle Pap and the Little Pap, two summits on Lochnagar itself. These are translations from Gaelic, since the name for the Meikle Pap has been recovered as *A' Chìoch Mhòr*, of exactly the same meaning [ə ciix voor] as Meikle Pap.

The burn that runs past the Royal Lochnagar Distillery is called the Distillery Burn, but had a number of different names: The Still Burn, The March Burn (from Scots *march* 'boundary') but was earlier called the Garchory Burn from Gaelic Garbh-Choire 'rough corrie' [garəv xoirə].

Loch Alvie

Inverness-shire (Loch-Alvie in c. 1591) [lox alvi]

This name is from Loch Almhaidh in Gaelic [lox aləvi], which itself is coined from the place called Alvie or Almhaidh. This name effectively has the same derivation as **Alloa**.

Loch Dhu

Although there are several places in Scotland with this name, this whisky does not seem to be named from any particular one of them. The name in Gaelic orthography is Loch Dubh 'black loch/lake'. The actual whisky is very dark in appearance, so this name may simply be reflecting that. For the spelling of Dhu, see p. 30.

Loch Donald

No such place as this exists in Scotland; it therefore seems to be an invention, from Gaelic or Scots *loch* 'lake' and the personal name Donald. There is a Loch Dhòmhnaill on Islay, which is simply the Gaelic for 'Donald's loch', but there is no evidence that this loch is intended, and the landscape depicted on the bottle does not resemble the place in Islay.

Loch Ewe

Ross and Cromarty [lox yuu]

The name Loch Ewe is now applied to a sea-loch, although some time ago it appears that the nearby inland loch that is now called Loch

Maree was once called Loch Ewe. In Gaelic, this is Loch Iù [lox yuu]. Iù is of uncertain meaning but may relate to an old word for a 'yew' coincidentally pronounced the same way. The modern Loch Ewe is mentioned in a song:

Tha dubharan sgòthach, 's na neòil, os ar cionn, a' roghnachadh dreach dhuinn, mu chladaich Loch Iù.

'Cloudy shadows, and the clouds, above our heads, selecting the hue for us by the shores of Loch Ewe'.

Loch Fyne

Argyll (*Loch Fyn* in c. 1591)

This is the name of a large loch in Argyll; in Gaelic, it is called Loch Fìn [lox feen]. The word *fìn* most likely from *fine* 'wine' a borrowing from Latin *vinus*. The idea behind this name might be that the water of the loch is like wine somehow. A Gaelic poem praising the chief of the Campbells describes him as *Leòmhann lonn Locha Fìne* 'the fierce lion of Loch Fyne'.

Loch Gorm

Islay (*Loch Gurym* in 1654) [lox gorəm]

This is the name of a large loch in the Rinns of Islay. Whilst this name can be translated as 'blue loch', it should be noted that *gorm* denotes a colour in Gaelic that has no precise equivalence in English. It can denote the blue of the sky, the green of grass, and is also the colour used to describe a person of African descent. It can also mean 'green' in the sense of 'inexperienced'. Loch Gorm is slightly odd because the form is not An Loch gorm, i.e. it does not have the expected definite article meaning 'the'.

Lochindaal

Islay (*Loch Nadal* in 1654)

This is the name of a loch on Islay which is either Loch na Dàla [lox nə daalə] or Loch an Dàil [lox ən daal], both meaning 'loch of delaying'; this is understood locally to be because the loch takes three-quarters of an hour longer to ebb and flow than Loch Gruinart

Loch Lomond

Dunbartonshire / Stirlingshire (*lacu Lummonu* in the eighth century) [lox <u>loum</u>ənd]

This iconic loch seems to take its name from the nearby mountain called Ben Lomond. Ben Lomond is Beinn Laomainn in Gaelic, and Laomainn derives from an old Celtic root *lumon* 'beacon'. Lomond Hill in Fife is of the same origin. They are both large hills which dominate the area, and would thus make excellent beacon hills.

Loch Lomond was considered one of the Wonders of Britain by an eighth-century author, who referred to it in Latin as *stagnum Lumonoy*.

Lochranza

Arran (*Loch Ransa* in 1654)

Lochranza is the name of a settlement on Arran which is itself named after Loch Ranza, a small sea-loch now used as a ferry port to Kintyre. This name comes from Gaelic Loch Raonasa; Raonasa is from Old Norse and was originally the old name of the river which flows into the loch here. In Norse, it was *Reynisá*, meaning 'rowan river'. Apparently, old remains of rowan trees have been found here.

Lochruan

Kintyre, Argyll (*L: Ruan* in 1747–55) [lox <u>ruu</u>ən]

This distillery in Campbeltown takes its name from a small loch to the north of the town. On modern maps, it is called Knockruan Loch, but earlier it was called Loch Ruan, which was in Gaelic Loch Ruadhain [lox rooəghin]. See **Dalaruan** for the meaning of the second element. This element also appears in the nearby Knock Ruan.

Lochside

Angus

This is first on record as Lochside Inn in Montrose. Ironically, this is beside Montrose Basin which is one of the few bodies of water in Scotland not to be designated a 'loch'. Doubtless, *Basinside would not have the same ring.

Longman

Inverness-shire (*Longman's Grave* in 1774)

Although based in Glasgow, this is presumably coined from the place in Inverness. In English, it is known as The Longman and in Gaelic as An Longman, with a definite article in both languages. Unfortunately, the origin of the name is unclear. The reference above to Longman's Grave was no doubt due to folk-etymology where the word was reinterpreted to mean a 'long man' who was thought to have been buried there.

Longmorn

Inverness-shire (*landa Morgund* in 1226)

The 1226 form above represents what would be written in modern Gaelic as Lann Morgainn meaning 'Morgan's enclosure' [lauN morǝkiñ]. *Lann* 'enclosure' is often used in a religious context to mean 'church'. In the sixteenth century, it was written as *Langmorne,* as if it were a Scots phrase meaning 'long morning'. The first syllable – now interpreted as Scots *lang* – was then changed into English *long*.

Longrow

Kintyre, Argyll

This is the name of street in Campbeltown and simply means 'long row'.

Lossit

Islay (*Lossit* in 1507)

This place on Islay is called An Losaid 'the kneading trough' [ǝn lositch], used figuratively to denote high-quality land. This name appears several times throughout the Highlands.

Lynch Isle

Lynch Isle is a limited-edition whisky distilled at **Clynelish** Distillery. There is no such place as Lynch Isle, rather it is an anagram of Clynelish!

Macallan

Moray

The name of the Macallan Distillery (established 1824) is taken by some to come from a building called the Church of Macallan, now situated on the grounds of the distillery itself. Various Gaelic derivations have been given for the name of Macallan, but there is no evidence for this name before the nineteenth century, despite oft-repeated claims of the name's antiquity. Thus, it seems most likely that the Macallan Distillery was coined from the surname, and then a story was constructed, claiming that the church coined the original name.

Machir Bay

Islay

This means 'the bay of Machir or Machrie'; in Gaelic, it is called Tràigh Mhachair 'the beach of Machair' [trai <u>vaxir</u>]. M*achair* is a word meaning 'a flat expanse of land', often denoting a sandy beach, as it does here. *Machair* has other extended meanings as well, such as 'golf links'; it is also the term for the southern Lowlands of Scotland, or the flatlands in the east of Scotland.

Machrie Moor

Arran (*Machremore* and *Machirbeg* 1445–50, that is, the big and small Machrie)

This means 'the moor of Machrie' where Machrie is a nearby place. This is from Gaelic Macharaidh [mexəri]. See **Machir Bay** above for the meaning of this element.

Mannochmore

Moray

Mannochmore seems to be a modern invented name. There is a Mannoch Hill in Moray which is really a range a few miles to the south of the distillery and it is possible this name was coined from that, with -more added on, as if from Gaelic *mòr* 'big'.

At the south of the Mannoch range is a place called Sidhean na Mannoch. Mannoch may come from Gaelic *meadhanach* 'middle' being a hill range between two places. Speculation could offer several ideas, but without further evidence, we cannot be certain of what the name may have originally meant.

The distillery takes its water from the Burn of Bardon, where Bardon is a settlement on that watercourse. Bardon possibly comes somehow from Gaelic *bàrd* 'river-side enclosure'.

Millburn

Inverness-shire (*Alt Moulyn nan Ry* in c. 1591)

This is a Scots or English name, now used to denote an area of Inverness, although it originally denoted the stream or burn here called Mill Burn (see p. 159). An old map of Inverness from around 1591, however, refers to Mill Burn as *Alt Moulyn nan Ry*; this is clearly Gaelic for Allt Muileann an Rìgh 'the burn of the King's mill' or 'Mill Burn of the king' [auLt muleN ən rii]. Its regal associations came about because this burn was used to drive the mills whose site was granted to the townsfolk by royal charter.

Miltonduff

Moray

This is a Scots name, meaning the 'mill farm of a man called Duff'. Milton is from Scots *miln* 'mill' and *toon* or *town* 'farm'. Duff is the surname of the erstwhile owner, who was most likely James Duff, 4th Earl of Fife (1776–1857), and a member of parliament. Before Duff's time, the name appears on maps as Milton Brodie or simply as Milton. See also **Dufftown**.

Moffat

Dumfries and Galloway (*Moffeth* in 1194) [mofət]

This name is of obscure origin. It is almost certainly of Celtic derivation, rather than Scots, but more than that we cannot say.

Moidart

Lochaber (*Mudewort* in 1346–72) [moidart]

The name of this large region in the eastern mainland of Scotland is from Gaelic Mùideart [muujarsht]. This name is of Old Norse origin, possibly from *Móteiðfjorð* 'the fjord of the meeting-place isthmus', perhaps relating to the place where Castle Tioram stands.

(Old) Montrose

Angus (*Munros* in c. 1178)

Montrose in Angus is from Gaelic Mon Rois 'moor of (the) cape' [mon rosh]. Old Montrose is a somewhat different settlement on the other side of Montrose Basin. Whether this whisky relates to this settlement specifically is unknown.

Mortlach

Moray (*Murthlak* in 1574)

This is from Gaelic Mòrlaich [moorlic], contracted from a longer Mòrthulaich 'big hill' [moor hulic].

Mossburn

Scottish Borders (*Moseburnford* 1747–55)

This whisky is coined from Mossburn House, in Jedburgh in the Scottish Borders, where the company is based. Moss Burn flows near the house, and further afield is Mossburnford, which is a bridge across the burn. Old maps also show a Moss-side in the area. The name is Scots in origin from *moss* '(peat)bog' and *burn* 'stream' (see p. 159).

Mosstowie

Moray (*Mosstowy* in c. 1591)

This is a difficult name to analyse. Most likely Moss- represent either Scots *moss* meaning a 'peat bog' or perhaps that word loaned into Gaelic. *Towie* may well be Gaelic *Tollaidh* 'place full of holes' [toLi]. The name is now in a Scots-speaking area, and often in Scots an -l- is pronounced as a -w- or dropped altogether; for instance, *wall* is often pronounced *waa* in Scots. Such a sound change may have happened in this name. Thus, the name could mean 'peat bog of the place full of holes'. We cannot be sure, however.

Muir of Ord

Ross and Cromarty

Muir of Ord is a Scots name, from *muir* 'moorland' with Ord, which is an existing place-name. See **Glen Ord** for a discussion of that name. In Gaelic, this name is completely different: Am Blàr Dubh 'the black moor' [əm blaar duu].

Mulben Moor

Moray (*Mulben* in 1493)

This name appears on Murray McDavid Mystery Malt, and the back of the bottle says it takes its name from 'shallow ford across the red stream'. This explanation is that which is supposed to be applied to **Auchroisk**. Mulben was understood to mean Am Muileann Bàn 'the white mill' in Gaelic [əm muləN baan]. In origin however, it may have related to other Gaelic elements, possibly *Maol-bheinn* 'bald mountain' [mwl veiñ].

(Old) Mull

Hebrides

The Isle of Mull, a large island in the Hebrides, has an ancient name of unclear provenance. It is on record as far back as AD 50 as *Malaios*. Several theories have been put forward for the original meaning of the name, perhaps the most sensible is that from Old Celtic *malo- 'rising, prominent'. In modern Gaelic, the island is called either An t-Eilean Muileach [ən tchelan mulox] or Eilean Mhuile [elən vulə].

North Esk

See **Glenesk**.

North of Scotland

This is rather an odd name for a whisky from a distillery in Cambus, near Alloa, Clackmannanshire, which many would not consider the north of Scotland at all.

North Port

Angus

Although *port* denotes a harbour in English and Gaelic, in Scots, it can also denote a gateway through a city wall. Thus, in Brechin, this means 'the north entrance'. The same element appears in the name of Westport in Edinburgh.

Oban

Inverness-shire (*Oban* in 1747–55)

Oban is in Gaelic An t-Òban 'the little bay' [ən t̯o͟opan]. Gaelic òb 'bay' (whence this name comes) is a loan word from Old Norse *hópr* 'bay'. Many Gaelic words to do with the sea are borrowed from Norse. Oban was a fishing village in the eighteenth century.

The text on the whisky bottle claims 'The first settlers arrived on the mainland in 5,000 BC and sheltered in the natural caves of the land then known as "an ob". This is presumably a reference to Distillery Cave in Oban. We do not know what language the first settlers in the area spoke, so we cannot know what they called the cave. That they used a Norse loan word in Gaelic is impossible, however.

The water source for this distillery is Loch Gleann a' Bhearraidh, a Gaelic name meaning 'the loch of Gleann a' Bhearraidh'. There is no such place simply as Gleann a' Bhearraidh on maps, but the name would mean something like 'the glen of the shearing or cutting'.

Ochterglen

There is no such place as this in Scotland. Ochterglen is bottled with the whisky Glenturret, and near Glen Turret is a place called Ochtertyre, so it seems that Ochterglen is a portmanteau word combining Ochtertyre and Glen Turret.

PORTMANTEAU NAMES

A portmanteau is a new word created from splicing parts of existing words together, thus *smog* is a portmanteau of *smoke* and *fog*. A handful of names of whiskies appear to be portmanteaus of other whisky names or place-names: Auchenhame, Caermory, Ochterglen and Tamifroyg appear to be such constructions. In general, portmanteau place-names are a result of artificial generation. For example, Cal-Nev-Ari was invented in the 1960s in the United States; it is created from the names California, Nevada and Arizona as it sits on the meeting point of those three states.

Octomore

Islay (*Ouchtmor* in 1507)

This is a Gaelic name: An t-Ochdamh Mòr 'the big eighth' [ən toxkəv moor]. It refers to a piece of land divided into eight. Several other similar names are nearby, but they do not number eight: An t-Ochdamh Fada 'the long eighth' [ən toxkəv fatə]; Octovullin or Ochdamh a' Mhuilinn 'the eighth of the mill' [ən toxkəv ə vuliñ] and An t-Ochdamh Meadhan 'the middle eighth' [ən toxkəv me-in]. A recent rebranding of the bottle now has the Gaelic form of this name on the bottle as 'Ochdamh-mòr'.

Old Ballantruan

Moray (*Balintrowan* in c. 1591)

This is from Gaelic Baile an t-Sruthain 'the farm of the streamlet', pronounced [bal ən tr<u>oo</u>-ən]. The stream is fed by Fuaran na Cloiche 'the spring of the stone' [f<u>u</u>əran nə kloicə]. The word 'old' in the name refers only to the length of time for which this whisky is matured.

Old Bridge

Inverness-shire

The label on back of this bottle says: 'The Old Bridge crosses the river Dulnan'. This river flows into the River Spey and there are several bridges over the river Dulnan, but the one in a village called Carrbridge is called the Old Bridge. It was built in 1717 making it one of the oldest stone bridges in the Highlands.

Old Elgin

Moray (*Elgin* in 1264)

The origin of the name of the town of Elgin is not clear; in Gaelic, it is Eilginn, and it is probably from this language that the name derives. Possibly it means 'Little Ireland' in the same way that we have names such as 'Little China' in New York. (See **Blair Atholl** for an equivalent development.) Other places in Scotland such as Glen Elg have the same element. 'Old' in this name refers to the original site of Elgin; New Elgin is a more recent development situated to the south.

The Old Man of Hoy

Orkney (*the Old Man of Hoy* in 1774)

This is a famous sea-stack off the coast of the Isle of Hoy, in Orkney. Created relatively recently by coastal erosion, it is said to resemble an old man at certain angles. This stack is on the coast of Hoy, one of the larger islands in the Orkney archipelago. This is a Norse name from *Ha-øy* 'high island'. Previously, the stack was known to local fishermen as Stawert, likely from an Orcadian Scots word borrowed from Old Norse *staurr* 'post, pole, stake'.

Old Pulteney

Caithness

This is not strictly a place-name; Old Pulteney is named after Pulteneytown, an area of Wick in Caithness. This itself is named after Sir William Pulteney (1729–1805) a member of parliament and a wealthy landowner. The word 'Old' in the name relates to the whisky itself. Pulteney as a surname comes from a place in Leicestershire, England.

The water source for this distillery is Loch Hempriggs. This loch has had a number of names over the years, but currently it is named after Hempriggs House. Hempriggs is a Scots name which denotes an 'arable strip where hemp was grown'.

(Old) Rhosdhu

See **Rhosdhu**.

Ord

See **Glen Ord**, of which this is a variant.

Parkmore

Moray

This is a Gaelic name in origin: A' Phàirc Mhòr meaning 'the large field' [ə farxk voor]. Gaelic *pàirc* is a loan word from Scots *park* or *perk* which can mean either a 'park' in the English sense or it can denote a 'field'. Originally there was probably a place called A' Phàirc 'the field' here, which was subdivided into *mòr* 'large' and *beag* 'small'. Nearby is Parkbeg which represents Gaelic A' Phàirc Bheag 'the little field' [ə farxk vek]. Parkmore was further subdivided in Scots-speaking times so that one eighteenth-century map shows three settlements Parkmor, Little Parkmor and Parkbeg!

Perth (Royal)

Perthshire (*Pert* in c. 1128)

The name Perth (or Peairt [pyarshtch] as it is called in Gaelic) is of Pictish origin, from an element *pert[h]* simply meaning 'copse'. Many Highlanders considered Perth and Perthshire to be the centre of Scotland, which gave rise to the saying: *bha an t-*àite *cho Albannach ri Siorramachd Pheairt* 'the place was as Scottish as Perthshire'. Perth was also believed, however, to be at the edge of the traditional Gaelic-speaking area, which is reflected in this proverb: *bho Pheairt gu Hiort*, 'from Perth to Saint Kilda'. See also the Wonders of Scotland on p. 136

THE WONDERS OF SCOTLAND

Three of the places discussed in this book also appear in a Gaelic proverb listing the wonders of Scotland. There are various versions of this, but the most famous one runs:

Trì iongantasan na h-Alba: Tobraichean Ghlinn Iuch, Cluig Pheairt agus Drochaid Obar Pheallaidh

The three wonders of Scotland: The wells of Linlithgow, the bells of Perth and the bridge of Aberfeldy.

Pinwinnie

North Lanarkshire (*Pinwinny* in 1747–55)

This name is probably Gaelic in origin. Names beginning with Pin- normally come from *peighinn* 'pennyland' and this name possibly was Peighinn Uaine 'green pennyland'.

Pitillie

Perthshire (*Piteily* in 1783) [pit<u>ee</u>li]

This small settlement just outside Aberfeldy is from Gaelic Peit Ìlidh 'Ilie's farm', where Ìlidh was probably an old personal name, perhaps the same name as that seen in **Roseisle**. See **Pittyvaich** for the word *peit*. Pitillie was also referred to in Gaelic as Baile na Mòine 'the town of the peat' [balə nə monyə], a common place-name for a place where peats were dug.

Pittyvaich

Moray (*Pitvaich* in c. 1591) [pitv<u>ai</u>c]

This is from Gaelic Peit a' Bhàthaich 'the farm of the byre' [pehtch ə v<u>aa</u>ic]. *Peit* [pehtch] is a Gaelic word that was borrowed from Pictish *pett*, 'farm', although it has now died out in the modern form of the language. In many cases, *peit* was changed to *baile* 'farm' [balə] in Gaelic names.

Pladda Island

Arran (*Flada* in 1549)

Pladda Island, or simply Pladda as it is known locally, is an island off the south coast of Arran. It is from Gaelic Plada or Plado which itself is from Norse *Flatøy* 'flat island'. Islands with names deriving from this form, sometimes appearing as Flada, appear several times around Scotland.

Pluscarden

Moray (*Pluscardyn* in 1226) [pluscǝrdǝn]

This is an enigmatic name in terms of pronunciation and original meaning, stressed as it is unusually on the first syllable. Most likely however, the name reflects a Pictish or early Gaelic name meaning 'nutshell enclosure' or 'nutshell-height'. (See also **Fettercairn** and **Urquhart Castle** for discussion of the element **carden*.)

Port Askaig

Islay (*Portaskog* in 1801) [port askik]

This is Gaelic Port Asgaig [porsht askik], from Gaelic *port* meaning 'a harbour' and an existing place-name Askaig, in Gaelic spelled Asgaig. This second word is a Norse name in origin, from *ask-vík* 'ash-tree bay'.

Port Charlotte

Islay

This harbour in Islay was named in 1829 after Lady Charlotte Campbell, daughter of the one-time owner of Islay, Campbell of Shawfield. The original Gaelic name was Sgioba [skyipǝ], now generally Port Sgioba [porsht skyipǝ]. *Port* means 'harbour' whilst *sgioba* in modern Gaelic is a term for a type of boat, itself a Norse loan word. As a place-name however, it may come from Norse *Skipá* 'ship river' although the watercourse is only a small stream here.

Port Dundas

Glasgow

This port in Glasgow was named after Sir Lawrence Dundas of Kerse (c. 1710–81), a Scottish landowner and politician. It was referred to simply as Am Port 'the port', by Gaels who lived in Glasgow.

Although not strictly relevant to the derivation of Port Dundas, the surname Dundas derives from the place of the same name near Queensferry outside Edinburgh. It possibly comes from Gaelic Dùn Deas 'south fort' [duun jes].

Port Ellen

Islay (*Port Ellen* in 1849)

This is in Gaelic Port Ilein [porsht iilin] or Port Eilidh [porsht eili], meaning the same thing as Port Ellen, i.e. 'the port pertaining to Ellen'. Ellen or Eleanor was the wife of Frederick Campbell of Islay (1798–1855) a Scottish politician. He also named Port Charlotte after his mother. The older Gaelic name is Leòdamas [lyootəməs] which is of Norse origin, meaning 'Leòd's moss', where Leòd is a personal name.

Port of Leith

Edinburgh (*aqua de Lyeth* in 1328)

Leith was once a rich district, distinct from Edinburgh. The name is coined from the Water of Leith which runs through it. For a long time, its port on the Firth of Forth was the source of its wealth, and although it no longer functions as a port, the name Port of Leith gives its name to several businesses in the area. The River Leith itself is of pre-Gaelic British origin, meaning 'damp' or 'moist'. Leith was known in Gaelic poetry by the epithet *Lite nan Long* 'Leith of the ships' denoting its position as a once-important port.

Portree

See **Seann Phortrigh**.

Port Ruighe

See **Seann Phortrigh**.

Pride of Strathspey

See **Strathspey**.

Putachieside

Aberdeen

Putachieside was a slum in Aberdeen which was demolished to make way for Union Street and Market Street. The original place was coined from another place called Putachie in Alford near the River Don, several miles outside Aberdeen. It later became known as Castle Forbes.

There are several places in the north-east of Scotland with this name or one similar. In each case, the name seems to represent a small stream running through a ravine. It is thus possible it comes from Gaelic *poiteachaidh* 'pot place pool' where the 'pots' represent small pools along the length of the watercourse.

Raasay

Skye (*Rarsay* in 1596) [<u>razei</u>]

The name of Raasay, an island off the Isle of Skye, is in Gaelic Ratharsair [ra-<u>a</u>rser] locally, although Gaelic speakers further afield refer to it as Ratharsaigh [ra-<u>a</u>rsai]. The name itself is not Gaelic in origin though, it is from Norse *Rárássøy* 'roe ridge island'. People from Raasay have the Gaelic nickname Na Saoithein 'the saithe fish'.

Rhinnesdhu

There is no such place as this in Scotland, but given that this is a Speyside malt, it is likely meant to denote **Ben Rinnes**, with the Ben removed and -dhu added. See the Ghaelic h which appears not once but twice in this name (p. 30).

Rhosdhu

Stirlingshire (*rosduue* in c. 1224–34) [ros <u>duu</u>]

This relates to the settlement on the shores of Loch Lomond called Rossdhu, from Gaelic An Ros Dubh 'the black promontory' [ən ros <u>duu</u>]. See also nearby **Inchmurrin**, which was known as Eilean an Rois Duibhe 'the island of Rossdhu' [elən ən rosh duuyə]. The name as it appears on the whisky bottle contains not one but two Ghaelic h's (see p. 30). The word 'Old' in the name relates to the whisky itself.

Rieclachan

Kintyre, Argyll

This distillery in Campbeltown was also spelled as Riechlachan in the nineteenth century, and this suggests a Gaelic Ruighe a' Chlachain 'the shieling of the clachan' [ruuyə ə xlaxin]. *Clachan* can mean a 'hamlet with a parish church, or a churchyard' – neither of which is likely here – or a 'small rock', which is more likely given the small place denoted in the name.

Rock Island

There is no such place as this in Scotland; this whisky blend was originally called Rock Oyster but was later changed to Rock Island.

Rosebank

South Lanarkshire (*Rosebank* in 1817)

This is a common name from Standard Scots English meaning simply 'a bank of roses'. The bank referred to is on the Forth and Clyde Canal. Nearby is Rosehill.

Roseisle

Moray (*Rossyle* in 1579)

Roseisle is a large district near Burghead, and old maps show a large loch which was once to the south of the area called Loch Rossil that contains the name in question. This contains Gaelic *ros* which means a 'promontory' perhaps denoting the large promontory now called Burghead. This element is also found in Pictish. The second element, written -isle in the modern form, cannot thus be from English *isle* but most likely derives from some Gaelic or Pictish term. There exists in a few sources a Gaelic/Pictish personal name written something like Ilei, so it may mean 'the promontory belonging to Ilei'. We cannot be certain, however.

Rosscanich

There is no such place as this in Scotland, most likely it is a portmanteau word comprising Ross and Canich. Ross in place-names generally comes from Gaelic *ros* 'promontory or wood'. Canich does not appear in place-names, however, although there is a place called Cannich in Strathglass.

Royal Brackla

See **Brackla**.

Royal Lochnagar

See **Lochnagar**.

Royal Strathythan

See **Strathythan**.

Rhuvaal

This is the site of a famous lighthouse on the northern tip of Islay. It is named after the promontory on which it sits, called in Gaelic Rubha a' Mhàil 'the promontory of the rent or tribute' [<u>roo</u>e <u>vaa</u>l], although it is unknown to what exactly this is in reference.

Rubha a' Mhàil

See **Rhuvaal**.

Ryelaw

Fife (*Rialie* in 1248)

This is a good example of a place-name not being what it seems. On the face of it, this looks like it is Scots *rye* and *law* 'hill'. This interpretation would be fitting for this whisky which is itself a rye whisky. The earliest spelling of *Rialie* in 1248, however, suggests a Celtic origin, and although several words could be suggested, the original element or elements denoted are not clear to us now.

In the sixteenth century, the word seems to have been reanalysed in a Scots context into the words *royally* and *royalty*. It is only in the nineteenth century that we see the modern spellings appear.

(Old) St Andrews

Fife (*Cinrigh Monai* in 747)

Although nowadays named after the patron saint of Scotland, some of whose bones it claims to possess, St Andrews has an older Gaelic name: the first element is Gaelic *ceann* 'head' [kyauN], followed by a Pictish place-name **Rymont*, later Gaelicised as **Righmhonadh*, as if meaning 'the end or head of the area called **Rymont*'. Pictish **Rymont* and its Gaelic equivalent both mean 'king's muir'; the muir in question is likely the area between St Andrews and Crail, part of which is still known in fact as Kingsmuir.

By the twelfth century, *ceann* 'head' had been reinterpreted as Gaelic *cill* 'church' (probably due to the place's ecclesiastical associations), so the modern Gaelic name for St Andrews preserves the original name as Cill Rìmhinn 'the church of Rìmhinn' [kiĩ riiviñ]. Further away from Fife, however, this name has sometimes been lost and forms such as Cill Anndrais are used, influenced directly by the present English form.

See also **Kingsbarns**.

St Magdalene

West Lothian [sənt madəlin]

St Magdalene was a farm to the east of Linlithgow in East Lothian, although it has since disappeared. The name survives in the same location as St. Magdalen's Road and in the name of this distillery. St.

Magdalene commemorates the biblical Mary Magdalene, who appears in many place-names.

A Gaelic Proverb about Islands

The following place-name proverb mentions three islands known for its whiskies:

Ceithir busacha fichead an Ìle
Ceithir àirdeacha fichead an Diùra
'S ceithir màmana fichead am Muile

Twenty-four busses on Islay
Twenty-four airds on Jura
And twenty-four mams on Mull

Busses, airds and mams refer to place-name elements. Many place-names on Islay end in English with -bus; these come from an Old Norse element *bólstaðr* 'homestead' (see Scarabus and Skeabost).

Aird- or Ard- is a popular element through the Scottish Highlands, including Islay; it comes from Gaelic *àird* 'height'.

Màm is the Gaelic word for a 'breast', representing a 'breast shaped hill'.

Sanaig

Islay (*Sandak* in 1507) [sanik]

Sanaig is on maps now as Sanaigmore. This name, better spelled as Sannaig [sauNik], is a Gaelic name of Norse origin from *Sandavík* 'sand bay', which is a common name in Scotland. See also **Glen Sannox**, which contains the same elements.

Scalloway

Shetland

This whisky is connected with a John Scalloway and Sons Ltd, so Scalloway here may be connected with the surname rather than the place. That said, this place-name is from Norse *Skálivágr* 'hut bay', where people would assemble for the law-courts called Tingwall.

Scapa
Orkney (*Scalpaye* in 1492)

This is a name of Norse origin, perhaps from *Skalpeið* 'scabbard isthmus' or possibly 'ship isthmus'. The exact import of the name remains a mystery, however.

The water source for Scapa Distillery is the Lingro Burn. Lingro is a farm name of Norse origin, from *Língróf* 'flax stream', perhaps originally applied to the burn itself.

Scarabus
Islay (*Scarrabolsay* in 1562) [sk<u>a</u>rəbus]

This is a name of Norse origin from *Skárabólstaðr* 'Skári's homestead' or 'gull's homestead', *Skári* being a personal name. This Norse place-name also appears as Scrabster in Caithness and Scarista in the Hebrides. This Norse form is passed into Gaelic as Sgarabus and then into English as Scarrabus, pronounced in the same way. It is usually spelled Scarrabus nowadays.

Scoresby

Scoresby is the surname of several famous people, the best-known being William F. Scoresby, a British Arctic explorer. His name both derives from a place-name, and is commemorated in a number of place-names. Which place this whisky denotes is unknown.

Seann Phortrigh (Old Portree)
Skye (*Portry* in 1654) [port<u>ri</u>]

Seann Phortrigh is the Gaelic form for Old Portree. Portree or its Gaelic version Port Rìgh [porsht ree] is a large settlement on Skye, and means 'king's port', although the original form may have been Port Ruighe 'shieling port' [porsht ruuyə].

Seggie
Fife (*Segghin* in 1207)

This name perhaps comes from Scots *segg*, 'sedge, rush', but we would not necessarily expect a name of Scots origin to exist in this area of Fife in the thirteenth century; we would normally expect names of Gaelic origin. In any case, the name looks to have been Gaelicised.

Seven Islands

This whisky was made for Indian markets, and the brand is owned by an Indian company, Tilaknagar, which is based in Mumbai. This city is built on seven islands, often referred to as the Seven Islands of Bombay. No doubt this whisky commemorates these islands.

Shieldaig

Ross and Cromarty (*Childaig* in c. 1591) [sheeldig]

The name Shieldaig in Wester Ross is from Gaelic Sìldeag, [shiildik] which itself is from Norse *Sildvík* 'herring bay'.

Singleton of Dufftown

Moray

See **Dufftown**. Singleton represents the fact it is a single malt.

Skara Brae

This famous site on Orkney was called Skerrabrae previously, often pronounced in the local Scots dialect as Styerrabrae. Most names on Orkney are Scots or Norse in origin, but we are not sure what this name means precisely. *Brae* denotes a 'hillside' in Scots. Skerra or Skara may be the same root as **Scarabus**.

Skeabost

Skeabost is a hamlet on Skye. The place-name is immediately from Gaelic Sgeitheabost or Sgèabost [skei-əbost]. This is clearly of Norse derivation, and whilst the second element is clearly *bólstaðr* 'farmstead' (See **Scarabus**), the first element is not known.

Skerridhu

This is a whisky that is distilled in Orkney, although there is no such place-name as this in Scotland. Cognates of the English word *skerry* meaning 'a sea rock just off the coast' exists in several of Scotland's languages, in Gaelic as *sgeir*, in Scots as *skerry* and in Norse as *sker*. Given its Orkney associations, this looks to be an Orkney Scots *skerry*. The second element, however, appears to be from Gaelic *dubh* 'black'. This is impossible as a name as there are no names of Gaelic origin on Orkney. Thus, the name appears to be a fabricated combination of Scots and Gaelic somehow.

Slochmor

Inverness-shire (*Sluch Muichk* in 1747–50)

This whisky is made by the **Tomatin** Distillery. Nearby this settlement, on the A9 are two places, a small settlement called Slochd [sloxk] and a narrow pass through the crags called Slochd Mòr [sloxk moor] on modern maps. It would seem that this whisky is named after the latter. Sloc or Slochd Mòr means 'big pit or cavity' [sloxk moor]. *Slochd* is simply an older spelling of *sloc*.

In Gaelic this pass was referred to either as simply An Sloc 'the cavity' [ən sloxk] or Sloc Muice 'the pig cavity' [sloxk muick]. This pass was important and well-known in times gone by as being the pass between Strathspey and Strathearn, meaning the summit between the catchment areas of the Spey and Findhorn rivers.

Speyburn

As with Glenspey, Speyburn is an invented name using the River Spey, see **Speyside** for the discussion of that name. This name sounds rather odd because the term 'burn' is used to denote smaller streams and watercourses, whilst the Spey is one of Scotland's longest rivers. See also p. 159.

The burn that feeds this distillery has different names for various stages of its course, but it is called Broad Burn as it passes the distillery and enters the Spey.

Speyside

Inverness-shire / Moray (*magnum et mirabile flumen quod vocatur Spe* 'the large and magnificent watercourse which is called the Spey' Latin text in c. 1200)

This means 'the sides of the river Spey'. Unlike **Glenspey** and **Speyburn** however, Speyside is a real term used outside the world of whisky. The Spey is in Gaelic *Spè*, pronounced more or less the same. Although the underlying meaning is often taken to be 'hawthorn' it more likely derives from an older Celtic root *skwei-*, meaning 'vomit', relating to Old Irish *sceïd*, and Welsh *chwydu*, with the same meaning. The idea would be that the Spey often floods its banks and overflows, which it indeed often does to this day.

Springbank
Kintyre, Argyll

This name is as it sounds, 'the bank (in the sense of 'river-bank') by the spring or well'. Campbeltown has many springs, which is precisely the reason why it once had so many distilleries. On old maps, a Springside Distillery is marked nearby.

There is no direct evidence that Springbank ever had a Gaelic name, but it is worth noting that nearby a part of Campbeltown is called Dalintober which is from Gaelic Dail an Tobair 'the bank of the well' [dal ən topər], a translation of this exists in a building in Dalintober called Springfield.

Spyniemor
Moray (*Spynyn* in 1203–24)

Although there is no such place as Spyniemor, there is a Palace of Spynie and Loch Spynie near **Linkwood** Distillery, where this whisky is made. This word is probably from Gaelic Spiathanaidh [spee-ahəni], itself from an earlier Pictish word, perhaps meaning 'hawthorn stream'. The -mor has been added later, as if from Gaelic *mòr* 'big'.

Starlaw
Falkirk (*Starlaw* in 1468)

This is a name of Scots origin, comprising *star* 'sedge' and *law* 'mound or hill', thus meaning 'mound covered in sedge'. Sedge grows best on boggy ground, and in medieval times the area around Falkirk was extremely wet. This name appears several times around Scotland.

STRATH

Names beginning with Strath- in Scotland generally derive from Gaelic *srath* (pronounced in modern Gaelic as [sra]). In Old Irish, *srath* meant a 'meadow or grassy place near a river'. In Scotland, however, it means specifically a 'broad valley', and this is the same sense that its Welsh cognate *ystrad* has. Given that Welsh and Pictish are very similar, it would seem that the meaning of *srath* has been influenced by Pictish, although the form has remained Gaelic.

Strathayr

Apart from a small street called Strathayr Place in Ayr itself, there is no such place as Strathayr proper in Scotland. (There is a farm in Tasmania called Strathayr; such coinings in Australia and New Zealand are not uncommon.) The name then, is most likely a portmanteau name from *strath* (see above) with the existing name Ayr.

The settlement Ayr (*inber-air* in 1490) was originally called in Gaelic Inbhir Àir 'the confluence of the River Ayr' [iñər aar]; The meaning of this river-name is unknown, although it is probably pre-Gaelic. The name of the settlement is one of a number which has *inbhir* in Gaelic (spelled in on maps as Inver-) but has since been lost. See also **Girvan**.

Strathbeag

There are various places in Scotland called Strathbeag, Srath Beag or Strathbeg. They all come from Gaelic (An) Srath Beag '(the) small strath' [ən srah bek]. As this whisky is a blend, it is possible that this does not denote any specific location.

Strathclyde

The River Clyde has one of the oldest Scottish names for which we have a record; the Egyptian geographer Ptolemy in AD 50 wrote it as *klōta*. It is always difficult to uncover the original intended meanings of large rivers in Scotland, but this name is thought to mean 'pure or cleansed one', a meaning possibly also seen in the name of the Cluden Water. For *strath*, see p. 148.

Today Strathclyde denotes a large region around the lower Clyde, but it was also the name of a kingdom from around 900 to 1100. Strathclyde in modern Gaelic is *Srath Chluaidh* [srah xlu-i], this name has changed little since 872 when it was written in the Annals of Ulster as *Sratha Cluade*. See also p 15.

Strathcolm

There is no such place as this in Scotland. It appears to be fabricated as if it were from Gaelic Srath Choluim 'Calum's valley'. See p. 148 for Srath. Likewise -colm appears for instance in Inchcolm 'Calum's Island'. Generally, the Colm denoted is Saint Columba.

Strathconon

Ross and Cromarty (*Strathconon* in 1309).

In Gaelic, this is Srath Chonainn [srah xoniñ]. Although the river flowing through the strath is now called the River Meig, it was likely once called the Conan. The derivation of this river-name is not certain, but it is certainly Celtic in origin and could mean 'dog river' using a descendant of the old Indo-European word for 'dog' seen in modern Gaelic as *cù* (plural *coin*), French *chien* and English *hound*. It should be remarked that the settlement of Cononbridge, however, is in Gaelic Drochaid Sguideil, meaning 'bridge of Scuddale' [droxitch skutchil], where Scuddale is a settlement name of Norse origin.

Strathearn

Perthshire (*Strathern* in 1264)

This is from Gaelic Srath Èireann [srah eiruN]. Èire or Èireann is an element that appears in several Scottish river-names and its meaning is not entirely clear. This is the Gaelic word for Ireland however, and it may be that these names were coined in the early medieval era as Pictish speakers started to speak the new fashionable Gaelic brought over at least in part from Ireland. The same thing may have happened in the name Atholl.

Strathenry

Fife (*Strathenry* in 1179)

Strathenry is from Gaelic *srath* (see p. 148) followed by a river-name. The River Leven in Fife runs past the lands of Strathenry and the landscape through which it runs fits the description of a *strath*. There is even an Enerly Burn in the area, and Enerly may represent the river-name as seen in Strathenry, possibly an earlier name for a particular stretch of the River Leven. Quite what form this river-name took, and what it originally meant or even what language it was coined in, is unclear.

Strathisla

Moray [strath ailə]

This distillery was originally called Milton Distillery on 1st edition Ordnance Survey maps. The modern form is an existing name meaning 'the strath of the River Isla'. For the meaning of *strath*, see p. 148. The river-name Isla exists several times in Scotland. It is pronounced in English as [ai-lə] and in Gaelic as [eelə]. The *s* is not sounded and was inserted into the spelling along the lines of words like *isle* and *island*. Its meaning is not known, but it is pre-Gaelic.

Strathmill

Moray

This is called Strathisla Mill on 1st edition Ordnance Survey maps (see entry above for **Strathisla**). It was then shortened to Strathmill, probably to avoid confusion with the new Strathisla Distillery.

Strathspey

Inverness-shire / Moray (*Strathspay* in 1590)

This is from Gaelic Srath Spè, the strath of the River Spey'. See *strath* on p. 148 and the **Speyside** entry

.

Strathythan

Aberdeenshire (*Aithe[n] Rivar* in c. 1591, i.e. Ythan River)
[strath i̱thən]

This name is derived from the River Ythan, with *strath* added on (see p.
148), although there is strictly no such place as Strathythan. Ythan is an
Old Celtic word in origin, from *iektona* meaning 'talking one' cognate
with Welsh *iaith* 'language', and possibly our English phrase 'yackety-yak'.

Stronachie

Perthshire (*Stronachy Hill* in c. 1796) [stronaxi]

This is clearly a Gaelic name. Stron- in names nearly always reflects
Gaelic *sròn* 'nose or nose-shaped hill'. The suffix -achy could be an
adjective meaning 'place of', thus the Gaelic form could have been
Srònachaidh 'place of nose-shaped hill' [sroonəxi].

Talisker

Skye

This is a name of Norse origin, perhaps from *Hallrsker* 'sloping rock',
which then passed into Gaelic as Talasgair [taləskər] or Talaisgeir
[taləshkər]. The distillery's water source comes from springs on a
nearby hill called Cnoc nan Speireag 'the hill of the hawks' in Gaelic
[krohk nə speirok].

Tambowie

Glasgow (*Tombouy* in 1747–55) [tambaui]

This is from Gaelic An Tom Buidhe 'the yellow hill' [ən tom buyə]. *Tam*
is the local pronunciation of Gaelic *tom* 'hillock', just as in Scots Tam is
used for the personal name Tom. See **Tamnavulin** and **Tamdhu**.

Tamdhu

[tamduu]

This is from Gaelic An Tom Dubh 'the black hillock' [ən tom duu].

Dubh means 'black', the spelling here of this element as -dhu is to make it look more Gaelic, see 'the Ghaelic h' (p. 30). For the change of Tom into Tam, see **Tambowie**.

Tamifroyg

There is no such place as Tamifroyg. The association of this whisky with the **Laphraoig** Distillery suggests it is a portmanteau word, using the syllable Tam- common in some whisky names, and a respelled final syllable of Laphraoig (which is often, erroneously pronounced *froyg*).

Tamnavulin

Moray (*Tomvulan* in 1747–55) [t̯amnəv̯ulin]

This name appears on maps as Tomnavoulin, which is from the Gaelic Toman a' Mhuilinn 'the little hill of the mill' [t̯oman ə vuliñ], thus the tagline given on the bottle of 'the mill on the hill' is more or less correct. For the change of Tom into Tam, see **Tambowie** above.

Tantallan

East Lothian (castri de *Temptalloun* in 1531)

This is coined from Tantallon Castle in East Lothian, although it is spelled slightly differently. This may be from a British *Dīn-tāl-ceμn* 'brow fort'. On South Uist, the name was remembered in Gaelic as Dùn Tallair [dun t̯auL̯ər].

Taranty

Angus

Taranty now exists as Taranty Road in Forfar. It is the Scots word for *trinity*, and doubtless celebrates the Holy Trinity.

Tarbolton

Ayrshire (*Torboultoun* in 1177) [t̯arb̯olton]

Tarbolton derives originally from an Old Scots place-name *boþel-tūn* 'maiden town', which later evolved into Bolton. At a later stage, Gaelic became prominent in the area, and *tòrr* 'hill' was added to the name, making *Tòrr Bolton. This name was reanglicised as Torbolton and then evolved into its current form: Tarbolton. This sort of name, which shows the ebb and flow of language and peoples, is quite common in Scotland.

Tarracroy

Moray

As a whisky, this is an alternative name for Aultmore and relates to a settlement written now on maps as Tarrycroy, a short distance from the Aultmore Distillery. The name is clearly of Gaelic origin, although the precise elements involved are not clear. There are a number of other names in the area also beginning with Tarry-, such as Tarrymount, Tarryfeuch, Tarryblake and Tarrieclerach. These probably all contain Gaelic *tòrr* 'hill'. Tarrycroy perhaps is perhaps from Tòrr na Craoibhe 'the hill of the tree', perhaps in opposition to nearby Tarrymount.

Teaninich

Ross and Cromarty (*Teaninich* in 1685) [tain̠inic]

This is from Gaelic Taigh an Aonaich 'the house of the hill or meeting-place' [tai ən wn̠ic]. *Aonach* is a word related to Gaelic *aon* 'one' and can mean a meeting-place where people come to 'one' place, thus a market place. Alternatively, it can mean a 'solitary hill' or 'upland region'. See also **Peninich** in the appendix.

The source of the water for this distillery is given in various sources as Dairywell Spring. This name is unknown outside works concerning the distillery, however. It appears as if this spring is what is called on the map as Tobar a' Ghàirdein 'the well of the arm' [toper ə gharshdin] This is situated near Culcraggie Burn which flows past the distillery.

Teith Mill

Stirlingshire (*water of Teth* in c. 1591) [tiith mil]

It seems there is no such place as Teith Mill strictly speaking, although there must have been numerous mills along the River Teith in Stirlingshire, after which this whisky is surely named. The **Deanston** Distillery is on this river. The Teith is another river-name which is very old and of obscure origin. In Gaelic, it is Teadhaich [tshe-ic]. The area through which it flows between Callander and Dunblane is called Srath Theadhaich 'the strath of the Teith' [srah he-ic].

Tobermory

Isle of Mull (*Tibbirmore* in 1540) [tober<u>mori</u>]

Tobermory is well-known in Gaelic as Tobar Mhoire 'the well of (the Virgin) Mary' [toper vurə]. This is the largest settlement on the Isle of Mull, built in 1788 as a fishing port. The well can be visited on a street behind the village, although the actual site of the original well was a short distance away. A story claims that it used to heal people who were mentally ill, until one day someone used it to treat a mad bull. The bull was cured but the well never cured anyone or anything ever again.

Tomatin

Inverness-shire [tom <u>atin</u>]

The name Tomatin is from Gaelic An Tom Aiteann 'the juniper hill' [ən tom ahtchəN]. On an old map from c. 1591, the name is given with a translation as *Tomm-Acken or Juniper moat. Moat* or *motte* is the Scots word for a mound, and seems to be a translation of *tom* 'hill',

The water used by this distillery flows in Allt na Frìthe 'the burn of the deer forest' [auLt nə friiyə]. A deer forest is a piece of land deliberately cleared so that deer can be hunted on it.

Tomintoul

Aberdeenshire (*Tomintoul* in 1747–55) [tomin<u>tuul</u> or tamin<u>tuul</u>]

This is from Gaelic Tom an t-Sabhail [tom ən <u>dowi</u>l] 'the hillock of the barn'. Tomintoul was the name of the highest group of crofts above Braemar.

Torabhaig

Skye [<u>tor</u>əvik]

This is ultimately from Norse þórvík: 'Thor's bay'. The name Thor was common in Old Norse, although it most likely relates to a person rather than the god. The Norse form was adopted into Gaelic as Tòrabhaig [toorəvik] and then as Torvaig in English [torvig]. The name on the bottle is almost correct Gaelic, although the o is long and should have an accent over it.

Tormore

Inverness-shire

This is Gaelic in origin, from An Tòrr Mòr 'the big hill'. The burn that flows past the distillery is suitably called in Gaelic Allt an Torra Mhòir 'the burn of the big hill', i.e. 'Tormore Burn' [auLt ən tora vooir].

Toulvaddie

Ross and Cromarty

This is from Gaelic Toll a' Mhadaidh 'the wolf's hole' [toL ə vati]. Although wolves have been extinct for centuries in Scotland, place-names from all the languages of Scotland show that they were once widespread.

Towiemore

Moray (*Towiemore* in 1690)

The name Towie appears several times across the Highlands of Scotland, and in the cases where the Gaelic is recoverable, the Gaelic form is Tollaidh meaning 'hole place' [toLi]. The element -*more* represents Gaelic *mòr* 'big' in contrast to nearby Towiebeg using Gaelic *beag* 'small'. Most likely there was an original settlement here called Tollaidh which was divided into two in Gaelic times. Later, when Scots encroached on the area Towiemore was further divided into Upper Towiemore and Lower Towiemore. See also **Mosstowie**.

Tullibardine

Perthshire (*Tulybardy* in 1337) [tʌlibardin]

This is a Gaelic name in origin: Tulaich Bhàrdainn 'the hill of the riverside place' [tuləx vaarshtiñ]. *Bàrd* is a Gaelic word which can mean either a bard (in the sense of poet) or a river-side meadow. The river in question here is the River Earn.

Because this place had an earldom, this name is mentioned several times in Gaelic poetry, for example: *Is ad shàr Iarl air Tulaich-bhearduinn* 'you are the excellent Earl of Tullibardine'.

This distillery takes its water from Danny Burn. The derivation of this name is obscure, but it is worth noting that the name flows through Glen Anny, so perhaps the original form of Danny Burn was *Allt Anaidh, where the final t has been reanalysed as an initial d- in the next name. The glen could have been known in Gaelic as Gleann Anaidh. What Anaidh or some variant might be however is unknown.

Tullichmhor

There is no such place as this in Scotland. Tullich is a place in Glenlivet, where this whisky was made and comes from Gaelic *tulach* 'hill'. Mhòr broadly speaking means 'big' although the *h* after the *m* here is not correct grammatically. In all likelihood, the -mhor was added to make the name sound more Gaelic. See p. 30.

Turnhouse

Edinburgh (*Turnhouse* in 1665)

The derivation of this name is not clear, but most likely it simply comes from the word *turn* in the sense of 'corner' with *house*.

The Tweeddale

Midlothian (*Tweddal* in 1147–50)

This is 'the dale, or valley of the River Tweed'. The Tweed is a large river that flows through the Borders. The Tweed is an old name and of obscure original meaning. See also p. 15.

Twin River

There is no apparent reason for the name of this new distillery in Banchory, there is no such river in the area. Possibly it denotes the twin rivers of the Don and the Dee in Aberdeenshire, which both flow into the sea at Aberdeen.

Uam Var

Stirlingshire

The original Uam Var reflects Gaelic An Uamh Mhòr 'the great cave' [ən ooə voor]. This is not actually a cave as such but a large cleft on a mountainside in Stirlingshire north of Callander, which was famous as a refuge for outlaws and robbers in times gone by. The form of the name Uam Var first appeared in Sir Walter Scott's 1810 bestseller Lady of the Lake. Scott was the foremost writer of his time, and was interested in Highland folklore, although he often took great liberties with names. He possibly changed Vor (how Mhòr is pronounced) into Var to fit the rhyme:

> 'And stretching forward free and far
> Sought the wild heaths of Uam Var'.

Uigeadail

Islay

This place is only seen in the name 'Ardbeg Uigeadail' and is coined from Loch Uigeadail, the loch on Islay which feeds the burn that runs through **Ardbeg** Distillery. Loch Uigeadail means in Gaelic 'the Loch of Uigeadal' [lox ukətil], where Uigeadal is a nearby place. The name is clearly of Norse origin, perhaps from *Víkadalr* 'bay valley', denoting the area through which Ardbeg Burn runs into the sea at a bay.

Urquhart Castle

Inverness-shire (*Airchartdan* in c. 700)

This castle is named from Glen Urquhart. Urquhart is from Gaelic Urchadain, from an earlier *Aircharden,* a combination of two elements *air* 'on' and **carden*. There are a number of place-names in Scotland that contain this second element. What it meant in the minds of the coiners of the place-names is not fully understood, but it is likely

Pictish in origin, borrowed into Gaelic, meaning something like 'encampment', thus Urquhart originally meant 'on encampment'. (See also **Pluscarden** and **Fettercairn**.)

Wemyss

Ayrshire (*Wemes* in c. 1180) [wiimz]

The Wemyss Whisky company is named after the Wemyss family, who themselves are named after the place called Wemyss in Fife. As a place-name, Wemyss ultimately derives from a medieval Gaelic word *uaimheas* 'place of caves' [ūəvəs]; *uaimh* is the Gaelic word for 'a cave' [uaiv]. The eponymous caves, many with Pictish carvings on the walls, are grouped along the shore north-east of the village of East Wemyss.

Whalligoe

Caithness (*Qualigeo* in 1619) [waligou]

This is written on maps as Whaligoe. The name is sometimes spelled Whale Geo which gives us a clue to the meaning; it is from Scots *whale* and *geo* 'gully'. Thus, the name means a creek or gully in the coast where whales might have been seen.

Wishaw

Lanarkshire (*Wischaw* in 1544)

This is a Scots name comprising *shaw* 'copse, thicket' with an uncertain first element, it could possibly be either Scots *withy, widdie,* 'willow' or *whit, whyt,* 'white'.

Wolfburn

Caithness (*Ulf Burne of Scrabster* in 1664)

This derives from the settlement Wolfburn in Caithness which sits on the banks of Wolf Burn, a Scots name of obvious derivation. The lower part of Wolf Burn is rather unhelpfully called Burnside Burn, after the nearby settlement of Burnside, which itself must have been named after Wolf Burn! To add to the confusion, the name Wolf Burn was not known locally; it was always called Howe Burn. See p. 159.

There are several instances of this name – both in Gaelic and Scots – and often there is a tradition that it was the site where the last wolf in Scotland was killed. If there was ever such a tradition associated with this burn, it has not been passed down to us.

BURN IN PLACE-NAMES

Burn is the common word in Scots and Standard Scottish English for a small watercourse, commonly referred to as a 'stream', 'brook' or 'creek' in other parts of the English-speaking world. It comes from Old English *burna* meaning 'a spring, fountain; a stream or river'. It is first on record in Scottish place-names as *Merburne* in c. 1170.

Because distilleries need running water to function, it is hardly surprising that many distilleries have the word 'burn' in their names, such as, Coleburn, Hazelburn, Millburn, Speyburn, Wolfburn. See also Black Burn, Ladyburn and Mossburn.

Wolfcraig

Stirlingshire (*Wolf Crag* in 1880)

Nowadays Wolfcraig is a single building on Port Street in Stirling. There is a plinth on it with a relief statue of a wolf with the words: 'Here in auld days / The wolf roam'd / In a hole of the rock / In ambush lay'. This recalls a popular local legend that long ago, a wolf woke a sleeping sentinel and saved the city from ruin by Vikings at the spot here, after which the rock was renamed 'Wolf Crag'. The Stirling Burgh coat of arms is described as 'the wolf upon ane crag' in 1624. Nowadays there is no crag to be seen.

Yesnaby

Orkney (*Yeskenibie* in 1536) [ẏesnəbi]

The final element of this name is most likely Old Norse *boer* 'farm', but the preceding element is obscure.

The Lost Distilleries
of Scotland

In the late eighteenth and nineteenth centuries, there were a plethora of small distilleries, many of which are mentioned only once or twice in print. As a rule, they simply took their names from the nearest settlement. In some cases, their exact whereabouts within the settlement are unknown. The following list comprises those named that the author has been able to identify. Where appropriate, grid coordinates have been given.

Achenvoir

NM957406?

Achenvoir was a whisky distillery that was open for two years from 1816–18 somewhere in Argyll. It is often assumed to have been situated on Islay, but the name looks to be from Gaelic *achadh* 'field'; whilst this is a very common element in the Highlands, it is not known on Islay. Therefore, the name must have been corrupted somehow or the distillery is unlikely to be on Islay. The other names listed alongside Achenvoir are all in Argyll. In the region of some of the other names is a place called Achinreir or Achanreir. We cannot be certain this is the place denoted, but it looks as if the name has been misspelled somehow. Achinreir is from Gaelic Achadh an Raghair meaning 'the field of the fallow land' [aχ ən r<u>w</u>-ir]. *Raghar* means 'fallow land, or land not in tillage'.

Babute

NR716495 Kintyre, Argyll

This was a distillery in North Argyll. There is no such place as this and it is only mentioned once in a list of distilleries, so it may well contain a typographical error. Balure in Kintyre is listed from 1817–37 as having a distillery, so in all likelihood, Babute is in error for Balure. This name comes from Gaelic Am Baile Ùr 'the new town'.

Baldarroch

NS651765

This is a lost distillery owned by a John Forrest somewhere in Stirling in 1828. In one record, it is spelled Baldannoch, but this appears to be a typographical error. It seems to have been called French Mill in 1821 and this gives us evidence of its location; there was a Frenchmill in Milton of Campsie on older maps. There is no place called Baldarroch in the vicinity, but a Baldorran or Baldoran is very close by.

Ballackarse

Inverness-shire

This was a distillery in 1816. Most likely it represents what is now called Balcarse near Kirkhill; this is a name of Gaelic origin from Baile Chars 'carse farm'. *Carse* was originally a word in Scots meaning 'low-lying land by water', but was borrowed into Gaelic as *cars* with the same meaning.

Ballagort

Stirlingshire

This is a lost distillery run by a John Zuill or Zuilt. Elsewhere this person is mentioned as owning a distillery at Blairgorts in Kippen, which presumably is the same place. It is now on maps as Wester Blairgorts outside Buchlyvie in Stirlingshire.

Balon W. Log

Perthshire

This name appears once in a list and appears to be 'Ballinloan, Wester Logierait', shortened for reasons of length. Ballinloan is indeed in Wester Logierait in Perthshire and is from Gaelic Baile an Lòin 'the farm of the marsh' [bal n loon]. The medial n was dropped in natural speech to make it easier to pronounce, giving a pronunciation close to Balon.

Bankell

For some reason, this is given in several books as a lost distillery, but Bankell is on the maps now in East Dunbartonshire, although previously it was part of Stirlingshire.

Barkmill

There are two lost distilleries by this name, one in Aberdeenshire and one in Perthshire. The Aberdeenshire one is perhaps the place now known as Pirriesmill outside Huntly. This place was mentioned by the Ordnance Survey surveyors as having a bark mill as well as a ruined (in 1861) distillery called Strathbogie.

The Perthshire name is most likely a description of the distillery at Dallerie west of Crieff. This was also mentioned as having a bark mill (amongst other types of mills) as well as a distillery in the mid-nineteenth century.

Boncloich

East Dunbartonshire NS6378

This is a lost distillery formed by a George Brown, Stirlingshire in 1825. Most likely it relates to Bencloich in East Dunbartonshire, which is nonetheless near Stirlingshire.

Cachladow

Perthshire (*Cockledow* in 1747–55) NN708237

This previously unlocated lost distillery is named after a now obsolete settlement which is marked on certain old maps just east of St Fillans in Perthshire. The name most likely comes from Gaelic A' Chachaileith Dhubh 'the black gate' [ə xaxələ ghuu].

Carnacumline

Aberdeenshire NO241943

According to records, there was a distillery of this name in Aberdeenshire in 1828, owned by a Charles Duncan; in 1831 it is spelled Carnacumline, which is probably the more correct spelling. Although we cannot be certain, the best fit for this name is Carnaquheen in Balmoral (*Carnachoun* (vel *Cornachowne*) in 1625). In all likelihood, -ml- is a typographical error for -h-, thus the proper spelling should have been *Carnacuhine*. Carnaquheen is understood today to be from Gaelic Càrn na Cuimhne 'the cairn of remembrance' [karn nə kw̃iñə], but the earlier Gaelic pronunciation suggests Carn na Cuine 'the cairn of the yoke, or obligation' [karn nə cuñə].

Cashside

? Aberdeenshire NJ721269

There is no such place known in Scotland and no other name in Aberdeenshire which could be appropriate. Cashside is perhaps the same place as Glenlogie, as records state Cashside was registered to a James Connan in 1826, whilst Glenlogie was registered to him in 1828.

Cashwell

This is referred to in several sources as Cushwell. The name Cashwell only appears once in a list that contains several typographical errors. It possibly represents Coshieville in Perthshire.

Caul

NJ326596

This is possibly Balnacoul which is by Coul Brae.

Corn Cairn

Aberdeenshire NJ5757

Corncairn (spelled as one word) is a region of Aberdeenshire that only exists on maps nowadays as a *burn* name, the Burn of Corncairn.

Coulis

This word most likely reflects Gaelic *caolas* 'strait' or 'narrow' [kwləs]. It appears anglicised on maps several times as Caoles and Kyles. Which particular one this is we cannot know.

Daside

Perthshire NN968143?

Daside is only mentioned in writing once as the address for an Alexander Bayn. There is no such place resembling this, and the name likely contains a typographic error. Perhaps the common place-name Damside was intended; several of these exist in Scotland. Damside House between Auchterarder and Aberuthven the most likely candidate.

Field

Caithness ND105654

Field is a common element in Caithness place-names, but there is no place called this without a qualifying element; it is, therefore, likely that Field is part of some longer name. Whitefield is the name of a small farm near to where Geise Distillery was known to operate in 1833, so perhaps this was a by-name of Geise. We cannot be sure, however.

Freeport

Islay

Freeport is the name of the area around Caol Ìle and Port Askaig on Islay. It was given by a local mining company but does not appear on modern maps. The Gaelic name for it is Ruadhphort 'red port'. See also **Caol Ila**.

Frenchmill

See **Baldarroch**.

Glendown

Lanarkshire

There is no such place resembling this name in Lanarkshire. The closest to it is Glendouran at NS8720.

Glenfarr

There is no such place as Glenfarr, and it probably represents Glenfarg, Perthshire (see **Aberargie**). The name only appears once in the list, which contains several other typographical errors (such as Auchenloshar for Auchentoshan).

Glenluig

Dunbartonshire

This is described as being somewhere in Dunbartonshire, near Arrochar, and between Arrochar and Rhu. There is no longer any such place, nor does it appear on any maps. Judging purely by the modern form, it might reflect a Gaelic Gleann an Luig 'the glen of the hollow' [g̊lauN ən luik].

Glentrodley

Aberdeenshire

This is also spelled Glen Trodby and is a lost distillery that was run in 1826 by Alexander Murray & Co somewhere in Aberdeenshire. There is no such place as either of these names in Scotland. Most likely the original form of the name was Cairntrodlie in Peterhead, and Cairn was swapped for Glen. Cairntrodlie as a name comes from Gaelic *càrn* 'cairn'; the second element is unclear, however. In Angus, there is a St Trodlin's Well, so it possibly relates to a saint's name.

Inverleven

Dunbartonshire

This distillery was in Dumbarton, at the foot of the River Leven. The name Inverleven here is not known before 1886. Thus, it is unclear if this is a *bonafide* Gaelic place-name, or if it was a later invention. In the early twentieth century, the Gaelic form Inbhir Leamhain [iñər <u>lewi</u>n] was recorded, which seems appropriate. The Gaelic for the River Leven is Leamhan which means 'elm'. Thus, Inverleven is 'the confluence of the elm river'.

Junich

Perthshire

This is a lost distillery in Perthshire, mentioned only once in a letter to a committee of the House of Commons in 1797. The other names in the list are all in the Pitlochry or Strathtay area of Perthshire, so it seems sensible that this is in this area too. There is no such place resembling this in the area; two names, however, have a part of their name containing something resembling this: Toberandonich is from Gaelic Tobar an Dòmhnaich 'the well of the Lord' and Donicvourich is from Gaelic Dùn 'Ic Mhuireach 'Murray's fort'. Whether Junich is a shortened form of either of these two names or relates to something else entirely is unknown.

Kinivaugh

This name looks to be one of a number of names that reflect Gaelic Ceann a' Bhàigh 'the head of the bay'; in anglicised form, it can be spelled Kenovay and Kennavay. This name is common in the Western Isles. The name beneath Kinivaugh on the list is Scarinish, a site on the Isle of Tiree which also has this name Ceann a' Bhàigh (spelled sometimes as Kenovay), so this site may have been intended. Several pieces of circumstantial evidence reinforces this. Tiree was well-known for having many distilleries at this time. A Donald MacLean, whom the records show as owning this distillery in 1819, is mentioned as living in this place in 1801. Finally, there is a name Baugh from Gaelic Bàgh 'bay', this odd anglicised spelling may have influenced the spelling of -augh at the end of this name.

Kinture

This name is mentioned once in a list as being in Argyll. Many other names on the list are from Islay. Kintour is on Islay and Kinture most likely is a variant spelling of this place.

Lenereach

Argyll NR224613

This is a lost distillery known to be in Argyll. The name is also mentioned in an 1837 list of baptisms, and the context suggests it is a place in Kilarrow parish on the Isle of Islay. There is a burn called Linne Riabhach [liñə ri̯-ox] in the Rinns of Islay which may be this Lenereach. This name means 'speckled burn', although *linne* normally means 'pool'. Alternatively, the name could reflect an otherwise unknown Gaelic Lèana Riabhach 'speckled meadow'. *Lèana* 'meadow' is a common element in Islay Gaelic, often accompanied by a colour term.

Lumbrane

Dunbartonshire NS392802

There was a Lumbrain Cottage in Alexandria by the River Leven in Dunbartonshire. Nearby is Linnbrane Hole, a pool on that river.

Middleton

Perthshire NN878143

This is listed as being owned by a William Gow somewhere in Perthshire. Middleton is a very common name, especially in Perthshire. Someone with the same name as William Gow is also listed as an informant for the Ordnance Survey to Middleton between Muthill and Auchterarder, thus this may be the place intended.

Milnamuir

Perthshire NO0419

Milnamuir is mentioned as a distillery in a text where it is owned by a John Balmanno who went bankrupt. This John and the place-name Milnamuir also appear in a horse tax roll of Aberdalgie Parish. The name is mentioned as *Mill of Muir* in another record. The name is from Scots *miln* 'mill' and *muir* 'moor' as in 'mill of moor'.

Monthlaing

This is mentioned several times in lists, but it is a typographical error for Mountblairy, since similar lists of distilleries exist but with the Mountblairy in the same position as Monthlaing.

Mount Keen

The name of this mountain is from Gaelic Mon Caoin [mon cwn]. *Mon* is an Old Gaelic word meaning a mountain, more or less. Caoin as it stands can mean either 'weeping' or 'gentle'. Most likely, however, this element is a reanalysis of something older, but we do not know what.

New Seat

Moray NJ523544

A place called New Seat is mentioned in a list of 1833–34 owned by a John Cook. There are several places called Newseat (spelled with one word) in Scotland, but there is only one in Elgin.

Orlan / Orlah

Perthshire

This is a lost distillery in Perthshire, mentioned only once in a letter to a committee of the House of Commons in 1797. The other names on the list are all in the Pitlochry or Strathtay area of Perthshire, so it seems sensible that this is in the vicinity too. In all likelihood, it is supposed to denote Urlar outside Aberfeldy. This is a name of Gaelic origin from *ùrlar* 'ground floor', here probably meaning a 'low flat area'.

Peninich

This distillery is mentioned several times in modern publications as being in Stromness, Orkney. Peninich would be an odd Orcadian name, however. A man called Hugh Munro is mentioned in association with this Peninich, but a person of the same name is known to have built Teaninich distillery at the same time. Therefore, it would seem Peninich is simply that name with the T- swapped for a P-. Such names as this are called ghost names.

Portliach
Ross and Cromarty NH753724

This name is mentioned only once in a list of distilleries in 1799. The context makes it clear that Portleich is intended, which is a place at the east end of Barbaraville in Easter Ross. It is from Gaelic Port Fhlich [porsht lic] 'wet port', there being no proper landing place here.

Rohean
Dunbartonshire

This is a lost distillery, listed once in a list in 1799 as being in Dunbartonshire. This is most likely Rahane in Gareloch.

Swadale

This name appears only once in a list that has several typographical errors in it. It most likely is supposed to denote Sordale, south of Thurso, which was previously spelled as Swordale.

Teabaggan / Tealaggan
Inverness-shire NH567446

This name is listed in several sources, but the original text clearly reads Tealaggan, which is a settlement outside Kirkhill.

Tendan
Perthshire

This is a lost distillery in Perthshire, mentioned only once in a letter to a committee of the House of Commons in 1797. The other names on the list are all in the Pitlochry or Strathtay area of Perthshire, so it seems sensible that this is here too. In all likelihood, it relates to Tyndun outside Aberfeldy (*Tayinduin* in 1753). This would make it very close to Orlah / Orlan if this is indeed Urlar. Tyndun is from Gaelic Taigh an Dùin 'the house of the fort' [tain duun]. It is at the foot of Dun Hill which in Gaelic was known simply as An Dùn 'the fort' [ən duun].

Tornabuiag

This place is also mentioned as Ternabuiag as being in the Ferintosh area, which is in the parish of Urquhart on the Black Isle. It is mentioned several times elsewhere in records, however, as Tornabuiag, always in relationship with Christopher or Christian MacRae or MacRaw. In one register, his name is given alongside Teanahaun, just outside Cononbridge. There were many distilleries around this area, so it seems likely the settlement was in this area as well. It is odd that the name is only mentioned alongside this person and seems to not exist before or after his time.

Ulgna More

Caithness

This is fairly obviously Olgrinmore in Caithness. Where -na is in error for -rin.

Wateresk

Angus

This is either an alternative name for, or has been subsumed by, Braeminzion in Glen Clova. Wateresk is coined from the River South Esk on which the settlement sits. See **Glenesk**

.

References

The references to early forms, as mentioned under the headforms, are in square brackets.

Aberargie   Beveridge, 1923, p. 3

Aberfeldy   [Fraser, 1926, no. 18] ainmean-aite.scot sv

Aberlour   [Moray Reg., 31] ainmean-aite.scot sv

Achenvoir   The House of Commons, 1819, pp. 903, 911, 913, 916, 918

Ailsa Bay   Watson W. J., 1926, p. 73; King J. (ed.), Robertson C., 2019, p. 88; Clancy, 2008, pp. 33, 43

Ainslie Brae   Whiskypedia, 2020, sv Ainslies

Airigh nam Beist   Macniven, 2015, pp. 157–58

Alloa   [ER i, 572] Watson W. J., 1926, pp. 502–03; Taylor S. et al, 2020, pp. 130–33

Annandale   Lawrie, 1905, p. 49; Watson W. J., 1926, p. 55; Chambers, 1843, p. 26

Arasgain   ainmean-aite.scot sv Erskine

Arbikie   [RMS iv, 2174]

Ardbeg   [Pont map 14]

Ardenistle   Macniven, 2015, p. 159

Ardgowan   [ER xi, 300] Dwelly, 1912

Ardlair   [Abd. Reg., 207]

Ardnahoe   [RMS iii, 1378] King J. (ed.), Robertson C., 2019, p. 408; MacNeil, 1900, p. 69

Ardnamurchan   Anderson A. O., 1961, p. 374; Watson W. J., 1926, pp. 93–94

Ardnave   Macniven, 2015, p. 288

Ardtalla   [Macniven, 2015, p. 134]

Arran   [CELT, line 340] Fraser I., 1999, pp. 9–12, 31–32, 135

Auchavan   [Roy] Diack, 1957

Auchentoshan   [Blaeu map Lennox] MacLean, 2014, p. 72

Auchinblae   [Arb. Chrs. no. 461] Taylor S. et Markus, G. , 2012, p. 297

Auchindoun   [RMS ii, 1997]

Auchnagie   [ScotlandsPlaces E106/26/4/63]

Auchorachan   [Pont map 73] Diack, 1957

Auchroisk   [RMS iv, 903] Pont map 61; Jackson M., 2004, p. 100; MacLean, 2014, p. 75

Auchtermuchty   Taylor S., 2010 sv

The Auchtertyre   King J. (ed.), Robertson C., 2019, pp. 127, 309

Auld Reekie   DSL sv auld

The Auld Brig   Lindsay, 1959 sv; DSL sv auld

Aultmore   [RMS iv, 1961] Pont map 9; MacLean, 2014, p. 79

Babute   The House of Commons, 1803, p. 654

Badachro   [Retours (Ross) no. 3] ainmean-aite.scot sv; Watson W. J., 1904, p. 163

Bad na h-Achlaise   Watson W. J., 1904, p. 163

Balblair   Watson W. J., 1904, pp. 25, 27

Baldarroch   The House of Commons, 1832, p. 1

Balgownie   [Spalding Club Aberdeen, 1845] Alexander, 1954, p. 15; Retours (Aberdeen) 313

Ballackarse   The House of Commons, 1819, p. 919

Ballaglass   Broderick, 1999, p. 41

Ballagort   The Scots Magazine, 1826, p. 509

Ballechin   [Blaeu map Scotiae Provinciae] Gow, 1899, p. 21; King J. (ed.), Robertson C., 2019, p. 271

Ballindalloch   [Pont map 32]

Ballochmyle   [Blaeu Gordon (Pont) 60]

Balmenach   [Roy] Diack, 1957

Balmoral   [ER v, 221] Diack, 1957

Balnellan   Alexander, 1954, p. 171

Balon W. Log   The House of Commons, 1803, p. 509

Balvenie   [Retours (Banff) 9] MacKenzie, 1865, p. 45

Banff   [Jackson, 1972, p. 80] Watson W. J., 1926, pp. 231–32

The Banks O'Doon   Lindsay, 1959, sv; Watson W. J., 1926, pp. 211–12

(Old) Bannockburn   Wade-Evans, 1944, p. 82; Am Fèillire, 1873 vi, no. 23

Barkmill   Ordnance Survey, 1845–1880 OS1/1/25/17; The House of Commons, 1831–32, p. 2

Barra   Stahl, 1999, p. 139; SSPN sv

Barrogill   Waugh, 1985, p. 288

Battlehill   Alexander, 1954, p. 168; Gazetteer for Scotland, 2020 sv

Beldorney [RMS ii, 1997] Alexander, 1954, p. 179; Ó Baoill, 1972

Bellfield Harris, 2002, p. 86

Benachie Robertson J., 1843, p. 538; Alexander, 1954, p. 172

Ben Aigen [Pont map 6(1)] Watson W. J., 1926, p. 502

Ben Aros Henderson A., 1915, p. 189

Benderloch [Pont text p. 84v.] Ó Maolalaigh, 1998, pp. 26, 28

Beneagles Haldane, 1929, p. 16; RMS viii, 1623

Ben Gullion [Roy] Martin, 2013, p. 173

Ben Ledi [Roy] Diack, 1957; King J. (ed.), Robertson C., 2019, pp. 50, 329

Benloyal [Pont map 1] Grannd, 2013, p. 60

Ben MacDhui Watson A. & Allan E., 1984, p. 16

Ben Morven Alexander, 1954, p. 338

Ben Nevis [Pont map 13] Meek, 1978, p. 165

Benrinnes [Blaeu map Aberdeen and Banff] Diack, 1957

Ben Royal Whiskypedia 2020, sv Ben Royal

Ben Wyvis [Roy] Watson W. J., 1904, pp. 102–03

Blackadder BPNR, 2020 sv; Nicolaisen, 2001, pp. 236–39; ODNB, 2021 sn

Black Cuillin King J. (ed.), Robertson C., 2019, p. 194

Bladnoch [ER viii, 257] James, 2017, p. 39

Blainrow logainm.ie

Blair Athol [RMS ii, 750] Watson W. J., 1926, pp. 168–29; Sinton, 1906, p. 181; King J. (ed.), Robertson C., 2019, p. 258

Blairfindy [Pont map 74]

Boncloich The House of Commons, 1826–27, pp. 11, 12, 22, 28, 31

Bowmore King J. (ed.), Robertson C., 2019, p. 402

Brackla [Land Tax Rolls: Nairnshire E106/23/4/3] Watson W. J., 1903, p. 54; ainmean-aite.scot sv

Braemoray [Pont map 8]

Bridge of Allan [Roy] ainmean-aite.scot sv

Bridge of Avon [Pont map 26] Watson W. J., 2002, p. 101

Brodgar [Thomson J., 1832] Sandnes, 2003, pp. 83–84

Brodick Bay [Fraser I., 1999] ainmean-aite.scot sv Brodick

Brora [RMS ii, 2506] Watson W. J., 1906, p. 361

Bruichladdich ainmean-aite.scot sv

Bunnahabhain ainmean-aite.scot sv; Macniven, 2015, p. 241

Burn O' Bennie [Gordon map 30 and 31] Watson A., 2013, p. 212

Cabrach [Blaeu Ross & Sutherland] Alexander, 1954, pp. 192–93

Cachladow [Roy] The House of Commons, 1818, p. 5

Calchou Williamson, 1942, p. x; James, 2017, p. 71

Cambus [RMS v, 636]

Cameronbridge / Cameron Brig Taylor S., 2010 sv

Campbeltown Loch Nicolaisen, 1970, p. 66; King J. (ed.), Robertson C., 2019, p. 335; Diack, 1957

Canongate [ER ii, 56] Dixon, 2011, p. 19

Caol Ila King J., 2011, p. 42

Caperdonich [Ordnance Survey, 1845–1880 OS1/12/18/99] Townsend, 2015, pp. 59–60

Cardhu MacLean, 2014, p. 19

Carnacumline [RMS viii, 838] Alexander, 1954, p. 194; The House of Commons, 1831–32, p. 2

Carraig Dubh MacDougall, 1934, p. 81

Carsebridge Taylor S., 2020, pp. 148–49

Caskieben [Lindores Chrs. no. cxvi] Alexander, 1954, p. 33

Clachaig MacKenzie, 1865, p. 38

Clynelish [Roy] Watson W. J., 1926, p. 93; King J. (ed.), Robertson C., 2019, p. 104

Cockburns BPNR, 2020 sv

Coleburn [Roy]

Convalmore [Roy] Diack, 1957

Corgarff [RMS ii, 3159] Alexander, 1954, p. 167; Diack, 1957

Corryhabbie [Thomson J., 1832] Diack, 1957; School of Scottish and Celtic Studies.

Corshelloch Diack, 1957

Coylumbridge Diack, 1957

Cragganmore Ordnance Survey, 1845–1880 OS1/4/17/76

Craigardle King J. (ed.), Robertson C., 2019, p. 254

Craigellachie [Pont map 6] Robertson Collection NLS MS397, p. 271; Watson W. J., 1926, p. 478

Craignure ainmean-aite.scot sv

Crois Chill Daltain King J. (ed.), Robertson C., 2019, p. 400

Cromdale [Pont map 61] Diack, 1957

Culdrain [RMS ii, 3599] Taylor S. et al, 2017, pp. 231–33; Personal communication with Simon Taylor

Cullicudden Watson W. J., 1904, p. 12; King J. (ed.), Robertson C., 2019, p. 148

(Royal) Culross Taylor S., 2010 sv

Culzean [RMS ii, 2626]

Cumbrae Castle [Gammeltoft, 2007, p. 484] Nicolson, 1882, p. 106

Daftmill Taylor S., 2010 sv

Dalaruan [Thomson] King J. (ed.), Robertson C., 2019, p. 335; Colville, 1943 (2009), p. 19; Martin, 2013, p. 255

Dalchully [Roy] MacBain, 1922, p. 274

Dallas Dhu [Moray Reg., 69] Lamond, 1995, p. 103; MacLean, 2014, 146

Dalrymple Bridge [RMS i, 381] Black, 1946, pp. 198–99

Dalwhinnie [Roy] MacBain, 1922, pp. 275–76

Dark Cove Master of Malt, 2020

Daside   The House of Commons, 1803, p. 507

Davaar   SSPN sv; Colville, 1943 (2009), p. 20; Martin, 2013, p. 14–25

Deanston   MacNiven, P., 2011

Deeside   Diack, 1957; Rivet & Smith, 1979, p. 338; Robertson Collection NLS MS397, p. 275

Dhoon Glen   Broderick, G., 1999, pp. 98–99

Dhunomhainn   [ER i, 1] ainmean-aite.scot sv Dunoon

Dornoch   [Fraser W., 1892 no. 4] Nicolson, 1882, p. 50

Drumadoon Point   Fraser I., 1999, pp. 78, 125

Drumblade   [RMS i, 942]

Drumlassie   [RMS iii, 2100]

Drumochter   [Pont map 25(2)] Sinton, 1906, p. 3

Dufftown   The History of Parliament, 2020; Gazetteer for Scotland, 2020 sv.

Dumbarton   Nicolaisen, 1970, pp. 84–85

Dumbuck   [Pont map 32] Campbell J. G., 1900, p. 270

Dumeath   Alexander, 1954, p. 266

Dunadd   [AU 683] Cox R. & Lathe, R., 2017

Dunaverty   [AU 712.5] King J. (ed.), Robertson C., 2019, p. 336; Joyce, 1910, p. 331

Dun Bheagan   [RMS iii, 2297] ainmean-aite.scot sv Dunvegan

Duncraggan   Macniven, 2015, pp. 243–44

Duncraig   [RMS iv, 204] King J. (ed.), Robertson C., 2019, pp. 129, 44

Dundee   MacFarlane, 1906, p. 357; ainmean-aite.scot sv; Nicolaisen, 1970, p. 85

Dunglas   Jackson M., 2004, p. 333

Dunnottar   [AU 681] Watson W. J., 1926, pp. 510-11

Dunnyveg / Dunyvaig / Dun Naomhaig   [RMS iii, 3085]

Dunosdale   [RMS iii, 2297]

Duntreath   [ER xi, 300]

Ebenezer Place   Guinness Book of Records, 2020

Eden Mill   Taylor S., 2010 sv

Edradour   Innes, C., 1855, p. 115; King J. (ed.), Robertson C., 2019, pp. 258–59; MacLean, 2014, p. 104

Ellisland   Williamson, 1942, p. 16

The Eriskay   King J. & Scammell E., 2019

Falkirk   Nicolaisen, 1970, p. 93; Nicolaisen, 2001, pp. 9–21

Fascadale   [Dorret, 1750] Henderson A., 1915, p. 158; King J. (ed.), Robertson C., 2019, p. 379

Ferintosh   [Blaeu map Ross and Sutherland] Watson W. J., 1904, p. 114

Fettercairn   [ER i] Watson W. J., 1926, p. 510

Finlaggan   [Acts, no. 21] SSPN sv; Watson W. J., 1926, p. 519

Finnieston   Muir, 1899, p. 84

Fleet Street   Mills, 2010, p. 382

Fochabers   [Moray Reg., 254]

Foinaven   [Pont map 1] Watson W. J., 2002, p. 70

Freeport   Thomas, 1882, p. 273

Friar's Carse   [RMS iv, 1658] Lindsay, 1959, sv

Gairloch   Watson W. J., 1904, p. 160; King J. (ed.), Robertson C., 2019, p. 163

Garnheath   Drummond, P., 2014, p. 404

The Gauldrons   [Roy] The Gauldrons, 2020

Gerston   Waugh, 1987, p. 68

Girvan   [RRS iv p1 no. 19]

Glamis Castle   Dunf. Reg., 210

Glenaden   [RRS v no. 261] Personal communication with Simon Taylor

Glen Afton   [Pont map 35(1)]

Glen Albyn   Dieckhoff, 1932, p. 182

Glenallachie   Watson W. J., 1926, pp. 478–79

Glen Ardoch   [Retours (Perth) no. 686]

Glen Bervie   Watson W. J., 1926, p. 489

Glenborrodale   [Langlands, 1801] Henderson A., 1915, p. 158; ainmean-aite.scot sv

Glenburgie   [Moray Reg., 77]

Glencadam   [Pont map 36]

Glen Calder   Watson W. J., 1926, p. 441

Glen Carron   Watson W. J., 1904, p. 192; James, 2017, p. 63; Robertson Collection NLS MS397, p. 151

Glen Catrine   Watson W. J., 2002, pp. 95–96

Glen Clova   [RMS iii, 494] Diack, 1957

Glencoe   [RMS ii, 2565] King J. (ed.), Robertson C., 2019, p. 360

Glencraig   Whiskypedia 2020, sv Glencraig

Glen Crinan   [RMS ii, 1464] Diack, 1957

Glendarroch   Barnard, 1887 sv

Glen Deer   Taylor S., 2008, p. 275

Glen Deveron   [Abd. Reg. 30] Watson W. J., 1926, p. 48

Glendouglas   [Pont map 17] Diack, 1957

Glendown   The House of Commons, 1831–32, p. 10

Glen Downan   [Roy]

Glendronach   MacDonald J., 1899, p. 204; Alexander, 1954, p. 292; Barnard, 1887, sv

Glendullan   Diack, 1957

Glen Eason   Fraser I., 1999, p. 159

Glenesk   Rivet, 1979, pp. 376–78; Diack, 1957

Glenfarclas   Diack, 1957

Glenfiddich   [c. 1591 Pont map 26] Watson W. J., 1926, p. 15

Glen Flagler   Encyclopedia Britanica, 2020 sv Henry M. Flagler

Glen Forres   [Moray Reg., 46] Watson W. J., 1926, p. 498

Glen Fruin   [Lennox Chrs., Addenda 4] Watson W. J., 1926; Diack, 1957

Glen Garioch   [Lindores Chrs. no. ii] Alexander, 1954, p. 285; Diack, 1957

Glengilp   Watson W. J., 1926, p. 512; Diack, 1957

Glenglassaugh   [Robertson J., 1843, p. 17]

Glengoyne   [Pont map 32]

Glen Grant   Glen Grant: A History, 2020

Glengyle   [ER v, 476] Diack, 1957

Glenisla   [Coupar Abbey Chrs., no. 127] Watson W. J., 1926, p. 513

Glen Keith   [Moray Reg., 25] ainmean-aite.scot sv Keith

Glenkinchie   [Roy] Watson W. J., 1926, p. 443; MacLean, 2014, p. 197

Glen Kindie   [Robertson J., 1843, p. 618] Alexander, 1954, p. 309; Diack, 1957

Glen Lairg   Sutherland, 1848, p. 18; Watson W. J., 1926, p. 522

Glen Leora   Mac na Ceàrdaich, 1879, p. 38; Richard Cox pers. comm.

Glenlivet   [Pont map 73] Diack, 1957

Glenlochy   King J., 2005

Glenlogie   Clancy, 2016

Glen Luig   Moss, 1981, p. 62

Glen Lyon   [ER i, 5] King J. (ed.), Robertson C., 2019, p. 294; Robertson MS NLS MS436, p. 6v.; Robertson S. &., 2009, pp. 306–11

Glenlossie   Watson W. J., 1926, p. 439

Glen Mac Clay   [RMS ii, 1096] King J. (ed.), Robertson C., 2019, p. 411

Glenmorangie   The Scotsman, 2003; ainmean-aite.scot sv Morangie

Glen Moray   [AU i 564] Watson W. J., 1926, pp. 115–16

Glen Nevis   MacCoinnich, 1908, p. 90

Glen Ord   [ER viii, 261] ainmean-aite.scot sv Muir of Ord

Glen Quaich   [Blaeu text Perth, p. 89] King J. (ed.), Robertson C., 2019, p. 303

Glen Ranoch   King J. (ed.), Robertson C., 2019, p. 265

Glenrosa   [ER v, 181], Fraser I., 1999, p. 19

Glen Rossie   Watson W. J., 1926, pp. 497–98; Taylor S., 2010 sv Rossie; Whiskypedia, 2020, sv Glen Rossie Distillers

Glenrothes   [ER i, 25] Taylor S., 2010 sv

Glenroy, House of   [RMS iv, 2346] ainmean-aite.scot sv

Glen Salen   Thomson J., 1832; Hannan, 1926, p. 16; King J. (ed.), Robertson C., 2019, p. 276

Glen Sannox   [Blaeu map Arran] Fraser I., 1999, pp. 129, 142; Diack, 1957

Glen Scotia   Colville, 1943 (2009), p. 19

Glen Shee   MacNiven, 2014, pp. 12, 35–36

Glen Shira   [Pont map 14] King J. (ed.), Robertson C., 2019, p. 334

Glenskiach   [ER viii, 594] Watson W. J., 1904, p. 89; MacLennan, 1974

Glen Sloy   [Pont map 17] King J. (ed.), Robertson C., 2019, p. 422

Glen Tarras   James, 2017, p. 348; Chambers, 1843, p. 31

Glen Torness   King J. (ed.), Robertson C., 2019, p. 231

Glen Torran   King J. (ed.), Robertson C., 2019, p. 203

Glen Tress   [Blaeu map Tweed]

Glentrodley   The House of Commons, 1826–27, p. 4

Glentromie   Pont text p. 138r

Glenturret   [RMS iv, 2061] Watson W. J., 1926, p. 446

Glenugie   MacFarlane, 1906, p. 70; Taylor S., 2008, p. 295

Glenury   Jones, 1867, p. 75

Glen Usk   Ekwall, 1928, pp. 151–55

GlenWyvis   Watson W. J., 1904, p. 100

Great King Street   Harris, 2002, pp. 286, 430

Hazelburn   King J. (ed.), Robertson C., 2019, p. 335

Highland Park   MacLean, 2014, p. 231

Hobbister   [Gammeltoft, 2001, p. 144]

Hoebeg   [Arrowsmith, 1807]

Holyrood   Harris, 2002, p. 314; Dixon, 2011, p. 17

Huntly   [Glas. Reg., xii] Alexander, 1954, p. 301; ainmean-aite.scot sv

Ila Insvla   Blaeu, 1654

Inchdairnie   Taylor S., 2010 sv

Inchfad   [ER viii, i]

Inchgower   Ordnance Survey, 1845–1880 OS1/4/26/122

Inchmoan   [Lennox Chrs., 25–26] Wodrow, 1701

Inchmurrin   [Lennox Chrs., 17] Lennox Chrs., 44

Inveralmond   Anderson M. O., 1980, p. 267

Inverarity   [RRS ii no. 152] Watson W. J., 1904, pp. 107–08

Inveravon   [Moray Reg., 77]

Invergordon   Watson W. J., 1904, p. 69

Inver House   Half Pudding Half Sauce, 2015

Inverleven   Watson W. J., 1903, p. 51

Islay   Anderson A. O., 1961, Broderick, 2013, p. 11

Isle of Harris   [Cameron, 1894, p. 172]

Jericho   Alexander, 1954, pp. xxxv, 305

Junich   The House of Commons, 1803, p. 509

Jura, Isle of   [Acts, 1]

The Kenmore   King J. (ed.), Robertson C., 2019, p. 314

Kilbride   Watson W. J., 1926, pp. 274–75; Macniven, 2015, pp. 157–58

Kilchoman   [ER xii, 319] King J. (ed.), Robertson C., 2019, p. 409; Henderson G., 1910, p. 196

Kildonan   [Retours (Bute) 18] Fraser I., 1999

Kilkerran   [RMS ii, 3136] SSPN sv; Watson, 1926, p. 278; Martin, 2013, p. 69

Killyloch   Whiskypedia 2020, sv Killyloch

Kilmartin Glen   [RMS iv, 826] Mac na Ceàrdaich, 1879, p. 419; Watson W. J., 1926, p. 291

Kincaple   Taylor S., 2010 sv

Kinclaith   Taylor S., 2007, p. 16

Kingsbarns   Taylor S., 2010 sv

Kininvie   [Retours (Banff) 9] Watson W. J., 1926, p. 502

Kinivaugh   The House of Commons, 1819, p. 913

Kinture   The House of Commons, 1819, pp. 914, 916

Kirkland   City of Kirkland, Washington, 2021

Kirkwall Bay   [University of Copenhagen, 2020] Nicolaisen, 1970, p. 10

Knockando   [Pont map 6(1)] Diack, 1957; Cooper, 1982, p. 106; MacLean 2014, p. 249

Lagavulin   [Langlands, 1801] MacCoinnich, 1908, p. 87

Lagg   Fraser I., 1999

Laphroaig   [Old Parish Registers 541/10 64 Kildalton] Henderson G., 1910, p. 194; Macniven, 2015, p. 174; Personal communication with Prof. Richard Cox

Largiemeanoch   Fraser I., 1999, p. 86

Ledaig   ainmean-aite.scot sv

Lenereach   The House of Commons, 1819, pp. 903, 911, 913; Parochial Registers of Baptisms 1820–1854, 2020

The Lincluden   [RMS ii, 22] James, 2017, p. 165–27

Lindores   Taylor, S., 2010 sv

Lingdarroch   Fraser, G., 1888, p. 1

Linkwood   [Pont (Gordon 23)]

Linlithgow   [St A. Lib., no. 28] Watson W. J., 1926, p. 384; King J. (ed.), Robertson C., 2019, pp. 39–40, 422f

Loch Alvie   [Pont text 137r] ainmean-aite.scot sv

Lochan Sholum   Macniven, 2015, pp. 175–76

(Royal) Lochnagar   [Blaeu map Scottish provinces] Diack, 1957; Watson A. &. Allan E., 1984, pp. 16, 72 & 105; Alexander, W. M., 1954, p. 284

Loch Ewe   Wentworth, 2003, p. 453

Lochindaal   [Blaeu map Islay] Thomas, 1882, p. 269

Loch Fyne   [Pont map 17] Watson W. J., 1922

Loch Gorm   [Blaeu map Islay] Dwelly, 1912

Loch Lomond   [Nennius] ainmean-aite.scot sv

Longman   MacLean, 2004, pp. 83, 85

Longmorn   [Moray Reg., 29] Pont (Gordon) 23

Lochranza   [Blaeu map Arran] Henderson G., 1910, p. 203; King J. (ed.), Robertson C., 2019, pp. 85, 412

Lochruan   [Roy]

Lossit   [Macniven, 2015, p. 273] Gray, 1939, p. 43

Lumbrane   The House of Commons, 1826–27, p. 5

Machrie Moor   [ER v, 197] King J. (ed.), Robertson C., 2019, p. 413

Middleton   Moss, 1981, p. 266

Millburn   [Pont map 8] MacLean, 2004, p. 85

Milnamuir   The Scots Magazine, 1788

Miltonduff   [Roy] The History of Parliament, 2020

Moidart   [Acts, no. 7] Cox, 2007, pp. 85–86

Monthlaing   The House of Commons, 1826–27, p. 4

(Old) Montrose   [Arb. Chrs., app. 1] ainmean-aite.scot sv Montrose

Mortlach   [RMS iv, 2360] Cooper, 1982, p. 90

Mossburn   [Roy]

Mosstowie   [Pont map 8]

Muir of Ord   Watson W. J., 1904, p. 110

Mulben   [RMS ii, 2189] Diack, 1957

(Old) Mull   Rivet & Smith, 1979, p. 409

North Port   DSL sv port

Oban   [Roy] p. 265; King J. (ed.), Robertson C., 2019, p. 345

Octomore   King J. (ed.), Robertson C., 2019, p. 405; Macniven, 2015, p. 343

Old Ballantruan   [Pont map 7(3)]

Old Elgin   [ER i, 1] Watson W. J., 1926, p. 231

Old Man of Hoy   [Lows, p. 1] Henderson G., 1910, p. 181; Marwick 1959

Old Pulteney   History of the Parliament, 2020; Waugh, 1985, p. 298

Orlah   The House of Commons, 1803, p. 509

Parkmore   [Roy, 1747-55]

Perth Royal   Lawrie, 1905, p. 117; King J. (ed.), Robertson C., 2019, p. 69; Watson W. J., 1926, p. 356

Pinwinnie   Drummond, 2014, p. 360

Pitillie   [Stobie, 1753] King J. (ed.), Robertson C., 2019, p. 317

Pittyvaich   [Pont map 61] King J. (ed.), Robertson C., 2019, p. 166

Pladda Island   Fraser I., 1999, pp. 138–39

Pluscarden   Clancy, T., 2017

Port Askaig   [Langlands, 1801] Macniven, 2015, pp. 277–78

Port Charlotte   King J. & Scammel, E., 2011, pp. 30–31; Macniven, 2015, p. 300

Port Dundas   Muir, 1899, p. 67; Taylor I., 2011, p. 130

Port Ellen   [Admiralty Chart 2515]

Portliach   The House of Commons, 1803, p. 654

Putachieside   Alexander, W. M., 1954, p. 105; The Doric Columns, 2020

Raasay   [RMS vi, 453] Henderson G., 1910, p. 130

Rohean   The House of Commons, 1803, p. 654

Rosebank   Grassom, 1817

Roseisle   [RMS iv, 2932] Clancy, T., 2004

Ryelaw   Taylor S., 2010 sv

(Old) St Andrews   Taylor S., 2010 sv St Andrews; King J. (ed.), Robertson C., 2019, p. 423

St Magdalene   MacDonald A., 1941, p. 119

Sanaig   Macniven, 2015, p. 348

Scalloway   Jakobsen, 1897, p. 114

Scapa   Marwick, 1952, p. 100; Henderson G., 1910, pp. 343, 348

Scarabus   [RSS v 1112] Gammeltoft, 2001, p. 144

Seann Phortrigh (Old Portree)   [Blaeu map Hebrides] ainmean-aite.scot sv Portree

Seggie   Taylor S., 2010 sv; Whiskypedia 2020, sv Seggie

Seven Islands   Encyclopedia Britannica, 2020, sv Mumbai

Shieldaig [Pont text 119r] King J. (ed.), Robertson C., 2019, p. 139

Skara Brae   Orkneyjar 2018

Slochmor   [Roy] Personal communication with Seumas Grannd; ainmean-aite.scot sv Slochd

Speyside   [Skene, 1867, p. 136] MacBain, 1922, p. 143; Watson W. J., 1926, p. 474

Spyniemor   [Moray Reg., 21] Watson W. J., 1926, p. 474

Springbank   Colville, 1943 (2009), p. 20

Starlaw   [RMS ii, 948] DSL sv star

Strathayr   AU 1490

Strathclyde   [AU 682] Rivet, 1979, pp. 309–10; Watson W. J., 1926, p. 44

Strathconon   [RMS i, Rob. Ind. 65] Watson W. J., 1904, pp. 149 & 280

Strathearn   [ER i, 1] Watson W. J., 1926, p. 168

Strathenry   Taylor S., 2010 sv

Strathspey   [RMS v, 1727]

Strathythan   [Pont map 10] Watson W. J., 1926, p. 211

Stronachie   Watson A., 1995, p. 159

Swadale   The House of Commons, 1803, p. 654

Talisker   Henderson G., 1910, p. 193

Tambowie   [Roy]

Tamnavulin   [Roy] Watson W. J., 1926, p. 423

Tantallan   [RMS iii, 1049] James, 2017, p. 251; MacDhomhnuill, 1984, p. 99

Taranty   DSL sv

Tarbolton   Scott M., 2003, p. 280

Teabaggan / Tealaggan   *London Gazette*. Part 2, 1844, p. 1654

Teaninich   [Retours (Ross) 141] Watson W. J., 1904, p. 76

Teith Mill   [Pont map 32] Watson W. J., 1926, p. 16

Tendan   [Stobie, 1753] Gow, 1899, p. 57; The House of Commons, 1803, p. 509

Tobermory   [RSS ii no. 3397] Calum Maclean Collection; SSPN sv

Tomatin   [Pont map 8] Diack, 1957

Tomintoul   [Roy] Diack, 1957; Watson A. &., 1984, p. 150

Torabhaig   King J. (ed.), Robertson C., 2019, p. 195; Henderson G., 1910, p. 189

Tornabuiag   The Carter Lineage, 2020

Toulvaddie Watson W. J., 1904, p. 47

Towiemore Francis J. Grant, 1904, p. 26

Tullibardinev[ER i, 26] Mac an Tuairneir, 1813, p. 70

Turnhouse Dixon, N., 2011, p. 184

The Tweeddale Lawrie, A., 1905, p. 158

Uam Var Scott W., 1810, p. 6

Ulgna More The House of Commons, 1821, p. 2

Urquhart Castle Taylor S., 2011, pp. 80–81; Anderson A. O., 1961

Wateresk Watson A., 2013, p. 89

Wemyss Taylor S., 2010 sv

Whalligoe Waugh, 1985, p. 420

Wishaw [RMS iii, 3045] Personal communication with Pete Drummond

Wolfburn [Francis J. Grant, 1902] Tobar an Dualchais

Wolfcraig Nimmo, 1880, p. 368

Yesnaby [Marwick, 1952, p. 157]

Infobox references:

Abers and Invers Beveridge, 1923

Auch- /Ach- / Auchter- King J. (ed.), Robertson C., 2019, p. 380

Fictional Whiskies Fandom, 2021; De Almeida, 2017

A Gaelic Poem about Campbeltown Loch MacDhunlèibhe, 1882, p. 67; Meek, 2009

A Gaelic Proverb Robertson NLS MS397, p. 211

Glens and Bens Donath, 2019

Nicknames MacDougall, 1934, p. 80

Strath Taylor S., 2011, p. 108

Tautologies Taylor S., 2010 sv Knockhill

Wonders of Scotland King J. (ed.), Robertson C., 2019, pp. 39–40

Bibliography

Abd. Chrs. Innes C. (ed.) (1845). *Registrum episcopatus Aberdonensis.* Edinburgh: Bannatyne Club

Acts Munro, J. M. (ed.) (1986). *Acts of the Lords of the Isles* (Vol. 22). Edinburgh: Scottish History Society. Blackwood.

Arb. Chrs. Innes, C. (ed.) (1861). *Liber S. Thome De Aberbrothoc; Registrorum Abbacie De Aberbrothoc.* Edinburgh: The Bannatyne Club.

Alexander, W. (1954). *The Place-names of Aberdeenshire.* Aberdeen: Third Spalding Club.

Anderson, A. O. (1961). *Adomnan's life of Columba.* London: Nelson.

Anderson, M. O. (1980). *Kings and Kingship in Early Scotland.* Edinburgh: Scottisch Academic Press.

Angus, W. (ed.) (1926). *Miscellaneous Charters 1165–1300* vol. iv, Third Series, 9. Edinburgh: Scottish History Society.

Arrowsmith, A. (1807). *Map of Scotland constructed from original material.* Retrieved from maps.nls.uk/joins/747.html

AU Mac Airt, S. (1983). *The Annals of Ulster.* Dublin: Institute for Advanced Studies.

Barnard, A. (1887). *The Whisky Distilleries of the United Kingdom.* London. Retrieved from scotlandfromtheroadside.co.uk/ebooks/whiskydistilleries. htm

Beveridge, E. (1923). *The 'Abers' and 'Invers' of Scotland.* Edinburgh: William Brown.

Black, G. F. (2004). *The Surnames of Scotland: Their Origin, Meaning and History.* Birlinn: New York. (originally published 1946.)

Blaeu, J. (1654). *Blaeu Atlas Maior.* Retrieved 2021, from maps.nls.uk/atlas/blaeu-maior/

BPNR The Berwickshire Place-Name Resource. (2020). Retrieved from berwickshire-placenames.glasgow.ac.uk/place-names

Broderick, G. (1999). *Placenames of the Isle of Man: Volume four: Sheading of Garff.* Tübingen: Max Niemeyer Verlag.

Broderick, G. (2013). Some island names in the former 'Kingdom of the Isles' revisited. *The Journal of Scottish Name Studies, 3*, 1–28.

The Calum Maclean Collection / Cruinneachadh Chaluim MhicGilleathain: (2020). *Mar a fhuair Tobar Mhoire an t-ainm / How Tobermory got its name.* Retrieved from calum-maclean.celtscot.ed.ac.uk/calmac/searchdetails. htm?story=uk011-01-09

Campbell, A. (1883). *Cartularium Comitatus de Levenax.* Edinburgh: The Maitland Club.

Campbell, J. G. (1900). *Superstitions of the Highlands and Islands of Scotland.* Glasgow: James MacLehose.

The Carter Lineage (2020). Retrieved from http://hugh-carter.com/HMC-o/ p2.htm#i59

CELT (2020). *Acallamh na Senórach.* Retrieved from CELT: The Corpus of Electronic Texts: celt.ucc.ie//published/G303000/index.html

Chambers, R. (1843). *Popular Rhymes of Scotland.* Edinburgh: W & R Chambers.

Ciobair, C. *Am Fèillire.* (1873). Inbhir Nis: Domhnull Friseal

City of Kirkland, Washington, *History of Kirkland.* Retrieved 2021 from kirklandwa.gov/Government/City-Managers-Office/History-of-Kirkland

Clancy, T. (2004). Philosopher-king: Nechtan mac Der Ilei. *Scottish Historical Review, 83*, 125–49.

Clancy, T. (2016). Logie: an ecclesiastical place-name element in eastern Scotland. *Journal of Scottish Name Studies, 10*, 25–88.

Clancy, T. (2017). The Etymologies of Pluscarden and Stirling. *The Journal of Scottish Name Studies, 11*, 1–20.

Colville, D. (1943 (this edition 2009)). *The place-names of the Parish of Campbeltown.* Campbeltown: Kintyre Antiquarian & Natural History Society.

Cooper, D. (1982). *Whisky Roads of Scotland.* Jill Norman & Hobhouse Ltd.

Coupar Abbey Chrs.: Scottish History Society. (1947). *Charters of the Abbey of Coupar Angus* (Vol. 2). Edinburgh: University of Edinburgh.

Cox, R. &. Lathe, R. (2017). The Question of the Etymology of Dunadd, a fortress of the Dalriadic Scots. *Journal of Scottish Name Studies* 11, 21–36.

Cox, R. (2007). The Development of Old Norse -rð(-) in (Scottish) Gaelic, in George Broderick and Paul Cavill, *Language Contact in the Place-Names of Britain and Ireland* (pp. 81--89). Nottingham: English Place-Name Society.

Diack, F. C. (ed. Dr. W. M. Alexander) (1957). Aberdeen University Special Collections MS2276. (unpublished manuscript by Alexander, of Diack's field notes. This document has no page numbers.)

Dieckhoff, H. C. (1932). *A pronouncing dictionary of Scottish Gaelic: based on the Glengarry dialect according to oral information obtained from natives born before the middle of last century.* W. & AK Johnston, limited.

Dixon, N. (2011). *The Place-Names of Midlothian.* Edinburgh: The Scottish Place-name Society.

Donath, D. (2019). Glen Buchenbach – Scotch Whisky?, in *The Trademark Lawyer,* issue 3, 2019 (pp. 100–01). Retrieved from edition. pagesuite-professional.co.uk/html5/reader/production/default. aspx?pubname=&edid=83d89d25-fae3-4000-88cd-f5710035fb6d

The Doric Columns (2020, February). *Putachieside.* Retrieved from http:// mcjazz.f2s.com/Putachieside.htm

Dorret, J. (1750). *A general map of Scotland and islands thereto belonging.* London.

Drummond, P. (2014). *Analysis of Toponyms and Toponymic Patterns in Eight Parishes of the Upper Kelvin Basin* (Unpublished PhD thesis). University of Glasgow.

DSL Dictionary of the Scots Language / Dictionar o the Scots Leid. (2020). Retrieved from dsl.ac.uk

Dunf. Reg. Innes (ed.) (1842). *Registrum de Dunfermelyn.* Edinburgh: Bannatyne Club

Dwelly, E. (1918). *The illustrated Gaelic-English dictionary:* Fleet, Hants

Ekwall, E. (1928). *English River-names.* Oxford: Clarendon Press.

Encyclopedia Britannica. (2020). Retrieved from britannica.com

ER John Stuart, G. B. (ed.) (1878). *Rotuli Scaccarii Regum Scotorum. (The Exchequer Rolls of Scotland) Series of Chronicles and Memorials 18 vols.* Edinburgh: General Register House.

Fraser, G. (1888). *Poems.* Wigtown: Gordon Fraser, and the Booksellers.

Fraser, I. (1999). *The Place-names of Arran.* Glasgow: Arran Society of Glasgow.

Fraser, W. (1892). *The Sutherland Book: vol. iii: Charters.* Edinburgh.

Fraser, W. (1926). *Miscellany of the Scottish History Society* (4th series, vol. 9) Edinburgh: Scottish History Society

Gammeltoft, P. (2001). *The Place-name Element Bólstaðr in the North Atlantic Area.* Copenhagen: C.A. Reitzels Forlag A/S

Gammeltoft, P. (2007). Scandinavian Naming Systems in the Hebrides in S. T. Beverley Ballin Smith, *West Over Sea: Studies in Scandinavian Sea-Borne Expansion and Settlement Before 1300* (pp. 479–95). Leiden & Boston: Brill.

The Gauldrons. (2020). Retrieved from Master of Malt: masterofmalt.com/ whiskies/douglas-laing/the-gauldrons-whisky/

Gazetteer for Scotland. (2020). Retrieved from scottish-places.info

van Gils, M., (2020). *Laphroaig Collector* Retrieved from laphroaigcollector. com

Glas. Reg. Innes C. (ed.) (1843). *Registrum Episcopatus Glasguensis.* Edinburgh: Bannatyne and Maitland Clubs

Glen Grant: A History. (2020). Retrieved from Campari Group: camparigroup. com/sites/default/files/brand/documents/glen_grant_-_history_eng.pdf

Gordon. R, & Gordon, J. (2019). *Manuscript maps by Robert & James Gordon, ca.1636–1652.* Retrieved from National Library of Scotland: maps.nls.uk/ mapmakers/gordon.html

Gow, A. (1899). *Cameron's New Historical and Descriptive Guide Book.* Aberfeldy.

Grannd, S. (2013). *Gàidhlig Dhùthaich Mhic Aoidh: The Gaelic of the Mackay Country.* Glasgow: Taigh na Gàidhlig Mhealanais.

Grant, F. J., (1902). *Commissariot Record of Caithness: Register of Testaments, 1661–1664.* Scottish Records Society.

Grant, F. J., (1904). *The Commissariot of Moray Register of Testaments 1684–1800.* Scottish Records Society.

Grassom, J. (1817). *To the Noblemen and Gentlemen of the County of Stirling...* Retrieved from maps.nls.uk/joins/679.html

Gray, A. (1939). *The History of Islay Place Names.* Glasgow.

Guinness Book of Records. (2020). *Shortest Street.* Retrieved from Guinness Book of Records: guinnessworldrecords.com/world-records/shortest-street/

Haldane, S. J. (1929). *The Haldanes of Gleneagles.* Edinburgh: W. Blackwood.

Half Pudding Half Sauce. (2015, April 14). *"Laurento", the Estate of Craig Biddle, Esq., Wayne, Pennsylvania.* Retrieved from halfpuddinghalfsauce. blogspot.com/2015 /04/laurento-estate-of-craig-biddle-esq.html

Hannan, T. (1926). *The Beautiful Isle of Mull with Iona and the Isle of Saints.* Edinburgh: R. Grant and Son.

Harris, S. (2002). *The Place Names of Edinburgh.* London & Edinburgh: Steve Savage Publishers.

Henderson, A. (1915). Ardnamurchan Place-Names. *The Celtic Review* (10(38)), 149–68.

Henderson, G. (1910). *The Norse Influence on Celtic Scotland.* Glasgow: J. Maclehose and Sons.

The History of Parliament (2020). *Duff, James, 4th Earl Fife [I] (1776–1857), of Duff House, Banff.* Retrieved from histparl.ac.uk/volume/1820-1832/ member/duff-james-1776-1857

The History of Parliament (2020). *Pulteney, William (1729–1805), of Westerhall, Dumfries and The Castle, Shrewsbury...* Retrieved from histparl. ac.uk/volume/1790-1820/member/pulteney-william-1729-1805

The House of Commons. *Reports from Committees of the House of Commons vol. 11.* (1803). The House of Commons.

The House of Commons. *Accounts and Papers of the House of Commons, vol. 14.* (1818). The House of Commons.

The House of Commons. *The Journals of the House of Commons vol. 74.* (1819). The House of Commons.

The House of Commons. *Accounts Relating to Distillation in England, Scotland and Ireland.* (1821). The House of Commons.

The House of Commons. *Accounts and Papers of the House of Commons, vol. 17.* (1826–27). The House of Commons.

The House of Commons. *Accounts and Papers of the House of Commons, vol. 34.* (1832). The House of Commons.

The Hydrographic Office of the Admiralty. (1795–1963). *Admiralty Charts of Scottish coasts.* Retrieved from maps.nls.uk/coasts/admiralty_charts_info. html

Innes, C. (ed.) (1855). *The Black Book of Taymouth: With Other Papers from the Breadalbane Charter Room.* Edinburgh: T. Constable

Inverleven Distillery. (2020). Retrieved from Difford's Guide: diffordsguide. com/producers/827/inverleven-distillery/history

Jackson, K. (1972). *The Gaelic Notes in the Book of Deer.* Cambridge: Cambridge University Press.

Jackson, M. (2004). The *The Malt Whisky Companion.* London: Dorling Kindersley.

Jakobsen, J. (1897). *The Dialect and Place Names of Shetland; two popular lectures.* Lerwick: T. & J. Manson.

James, A. (2017). *Brittonic Language in the Old North.* Scottish Place-name Society.

Jones, E. (1867). Correspondence. *Friends' Review: A Religious, Literary and Miscellaneous Journal, 21.*

Joyce, P. W. (1910). *The Origin and History of Irish Names of Places.* London: Longmans, Green & Co.

King, J. (2005). Lochy Names and Adomnan's Nigra Dea. *Nomina,* 69–91.

King, J. &. Cottar, M. (2011). *Place-names in Islay and Jura / Ainmean-àite ann an Ìle agus Diùra.* Scottish Natural Heritage.

King, J. &. Eilidh, S. (2019). *Ainmean-àite Èirisgeigh / Place-names of Eriskay.* Scottish Natural Heritage.

King, J (ed.) & Robertson, C. M. (2019). *Scottish Gaelic Place-Names* Sleat: Clò Ainmean-   Àite na h-Alba.

Lamond, J. & Tucek, R. (1995). *The Malt Whisky File.* Wine Appreciation Guild.

Langlands, G. (1801). *This map of Argyllshire.* Retrieved from maps.nls.uk/ joins/581.html

Lawrie, A. C. (1905). *Early Scottish Charters prior to AD 1153.* Glasgow: MacLehose.

Lennox Chrs. Fraser, W. (1874). *The Lennox: vol. 1* Edinburgh.

Lindores Chrs. Dowden, J. (1903). *Chartulary of the Abbey of Lindores 1195– 1479* vol. xlii. Edinburgh: Scottish History Society.

Lindsay, M. (1959). *Burns Encyclopedia*: Retrieved from robertburns.org/ encyclopedia logainm.ie (2020). Placenames Database of Ireland. Retrieved from logainm. ie/

London Gazette. Part 2. (1844).

Low, G. (1879). *A tour through the islands of Orkney and Schetland: containing hints relative to their ancient, modern, and natural history, collected in 1774.* Kirkwall: William Peace & Son

Mac an Tuairneir, P. (1813). *Comhchruinneacha do dhòrain taghta, Ghàidhealach.* Edinburgh: T. Stiubhard.

Mac na Ceàrdaich, G. (1879). *The Gaelic Songster: An t-Òranaiche.* Glasgow: Archibald Sinclair.

MacBain, A. (1922). *Place names, Highlands & islands of Scotland.* Stirling: E. MacKay.

MacCoinnich, U. (1908). A Measg Tuath na Gaidhealtachd. In *The Old Highlands: Being Papers Read Before the Gaelic Society of Glasgow, 1895–1906.*

MacDhomhnuill, A. I. (1984). *The Hebridean Connection: Eachdruidhean agus Sgeulachdan bho Sheanachaidhean Uidhist.* Halifax: John Dyell Co.

MacDhunlèibhe, U. (1822). *Duain agus Òrain.* Glasgow: Archibald Sinclair.

MacDonald, A. (1941). *The Place-names of West Lothian.* Edinburgh: Oliver & Boyd.

MacDonald, J. (1899). *Place Names of West Aberdeenshire.* Aberdeen: New Spalding Club.

MacDougall, H. (1934). Far-Ainmean is Inisgean nan Gàidheal in *The Active Gael*, pp. 68–94.

MacFarlane, W. (ed.) (1906). *Geographical Collections Relating to Scotland Made by Walter Macfarlane.* Edinburgh: Scottish History Society.

MacKenzie, J. (1865). *Sàr-Obair nam Bàrd Gaelach or, the Beauties of Gaelic Poetry.* Glasgow: MacGregor, Polson & Co.

MacLean, C. (2014). *Charles MacLean's Whiskypedia: A Gazetteer of Scotch Whisky.* Edinburgh: Birlinn.

MacLean, R. (2004). *The Gaelic Place Names and Heritage of Inverness.* Inverness: Culcabock Publishing.

MacLennan, A. F. M. (1974). *Some Place-Names in Ferindonald.* Ross-shire Journal 4th Jan 1974.

MacNeil. (1900). *The New Guide to Islay with Maps, Illustrations, Place-names and sketch map of Machrie Golf Links.* Glasgow: Archibald Sinclair

Macniven, A. (2015). *The Vikings in Islay.* Edinburgh: Birlinn.

McNiven, P. (2011). *Gaelic place-names and the social history of Gaelic speakers in Menteith.* (unpublished PhD thesis). University of Glasgow.

McNiven, P. (2014). *The Place-names of Glenshee: a preliminary study for the Perth and Kinross Heritage Trust.* Retrieved from Perth and Kinross Heritage Trust: pkht.org.uk/files/4315/2537/5533/GAP_theplacenamesofglenshee_pmcniven.pdf

Martin, A., (2013). *Kintyre Places and Place-Names*. Kilkerran: Grimsay Press.

Marwick, H. (1952). *Orkney Farm-names*. Kirkwall: W. R. Mackintosh.

Marwick, H. (1959). *The 'Old Man' in Place-Names*. In Saga och Sed: Festskrift til Dag Strömbäck

Master of Malt. (2020). *Ardbeg Dark Cove*. Retrieved from Master of Malt: masterofmalt.com/whiskies/ardbeg/ardbeg-dark-cove-whisky

Meek, D. (1978). *The Campbell Collection of Gaelic Proverbs*. Inverness: Gaelic Society of Inverness.

Meek, D. (2009). Making History: William Livingstone and the Creation of "Blar Shunadail" in *A Land that Lies Westward* (pp. 197–218). Edinburgh: Birlinn.

Mills, A. D. (2010). *A Dictionary of London Place-Names*. St Ives: Oxford University Press.

Moray Reg. Registrum Episcopatus Moraviensis. (1837). Bannatyne Club. Retrieved from archive.org/details/registrumepisc5800morauoft.

Moss, M. S. (1981). *The Making of Scotch Whisky: A History of the Scotch Whisky Distilling Industry*. Edinburgh: James & James.

Muir, J. (1899). *Glasgow Streets and Places: Notes and Memoranda*. Glasgow and Edinburgh: William Hodge.

Nennius. (c. 800). *Historia brittonum*. Retrieved September 2019 from intratext.com/IXT/LAT0936/_P7.HTM

Nicolaisen, W. F. H. (1970). *The Names of Towns and Cities in Britain*. London: B. T. Batsford Ltd.

Nicolaisen, W. F. H. (2000). *Scottish Place-Names*. Edinburgh: John Donald.

Nicolson, A. (1882). *A collection of Gaelic proverbs and familiar phrases based on Macintosh's collection. Edinburgh*: MacLachlan and Stewart.

Nimmo, W. (1880). *The History of Stirlingshire* (3rd ed., vol. 1). Glasgow: Thomas D. Morrison.

ODNB (2021). Oxford Dictionary of National Biography. Retrieved from oxforddnb.com

Ó Baoill, C.. (1972). *Bàrdachd Shìlis na Ceapaich: Poems and Songs by Sìleas MacDonald*. Edinburgh: Scottish Academic Press for the Scottish Gaelic Texts Society.

Ó Maolalaigh, R. (1998). Place-names as a Resource for the Historical Linguist. In Simon Taylor, (ed.) *The Uses of Place-Names* (pp. 12–53). Edinburgh: Scottish Cultural Press.

Ordnance Survey (1845–80). Ordnance Survey Namebooks retrieved from scotlandsplaces.gov.uk/digital-volumes/ordnance-survey-name-books

Orkneyjar (2018). Skara Brae. Retrieved from orkneyjar.com/history/skarabrae

Parochial Registers of Baptisms 1820–1854. (2020). Retrieved from http://homepages.rootsweb.com/~steve/islay/opr/text/Argyll%20Bowmore%20Killarow_Baptisms_1820-1854(2).txt

Pont, T. (c. 1591). Pont maps and texts. National Library of Scotland. Retrieved 2019, from maps.nls.uk/pont/index.html

Retours Thomson, T. (ed.). (1811–16). *Inquisitionum ad capellam domini regis retornatarum*. Edinburgh.

Rivet, A. &. Smith, C. (1979). *The Place-names of Roman Britain*. London: Princeton University Press.

RMS Thomson, J. M. (ed.) (1882–1914). *Registrum Magni Sigilli Scottorum (Register of the Great Seal)* 11 vols. Edinburgh: General Register House

Robertson, C. M., (1895–1927). Robertson Collection at the National Library of Scotland

Robertson, J. (1843). *Collection for a History of the Shires of Aberdeen and Banff*. Spalding Club.

Robertson, S. &. Dilworth, T., (2009). *Tales from Highland Perthshire collected by Lady Evelyn Stewart Murray*. The Scottish Gaelic Texts Society.

Roy, W. (1747–55). *The Military Survey of Scotland*. Retrieved from nls.uk/maps/roy/

Sandnes, B. (2003). *From Starafjall to Starling Hill* (unpublished PhD thesis). Norwegian University of Science and Technology.

School of Scottish and Celtic Studies, *Scottish Place-name Survey material*. University of Edinburgh.

ScotlandsPlaces. (2020). *Land Tax Rolls*. Retrieved from ScotlandsPlaces: scotlandsplaces.gov.uk/digital-volumes/historical-tax-rolls/

The Scots Magazine. (1788). Bankrupts. *The Scots Magazine*.

The Scots Magazine. (1826). Alphabetical List of Scotch Bankruptcies and Dividends, announced March 1826. *The Scots Magazine*, p. 509.

The Scotsman. (2003). *Tranquillity returns to Glenmorangie as Gaelic name challenge fails*. Retrieved from The Scotsman: scotsman.com/business/companies/tranquillity-returns-to-glenmorangie-as-gaelic-name-challenge-fails-1-1384046

Scott, M. (2003). *The Germanic Toponymicon of Southern Scotland: Place-Name Elements and their contribution to the Lexicon and Onomasticon* (unpublished PhD thesis). The University of Glasgow.

Scott, W. (1810). *The Lady of the Lake: A Poem*. John Ballantyne and Company: Edinburgh.

Sinton, T. (1906). *The Poetry of Badenoch*. Inverness.

Skene, W. F. (1867). *Chronicles of the Picts, chronicles of the Scots, and other early memorials of Scottish history*. Edinburgh: H. M. General Register House

SSPN Glasgow University. (2013). Saints in Scottish Place-Names. Retrieved from saintsplaces.gla.ac.uk/

St A. Lib. Innes C. (ed.) (1841) *Liber Cartarum Prioratus Sancti Andree in Scotia*. Edinburgh: Bannatyne Club.

Stahl, A. B. (1999). *Place-Names of Barra in the Outer Hebrides* (Unpublished PhD thesis). University of Edinburgh.

Stobie, J. (1753). *South East Part of Perthshire* (map).

Sutherland, T. D. (1848). *Two Ancient Records of the Bishopric of Caithness from the Charter-room at Dunrobin*. Edinburgh: The Bannatyne Club.

Taylor, I. (2011). *Place-Names of Scotland*. Edinburgh: Birlinn.

Taylor, S. (2007). Gaelic in Glasgow: The Onomastic Evidence. In S. M. Kidd, *Baile Mòr nan Gàidheal*. Glasgow: University of Glasgow Department of Celtic.

Taylor, S. (2008). The Toponymic Landscape of the Gaelic notes in the Book of Deer. In K. Forsyth, *Studies on the Book of Deer* (pp. 275–308). Four Courts Press.

Taylor, S. (2011). Pictish Place-Names Revisited. In Driscoll, Geddes & Hall (eds.) *Pictish Progress: New Studies on North Britain in the Early Middle Ages* (pp. 67–118). Leiden: Brill.

Taylor, S. et al. (2017). *The Place-names of Kinross-shire*. Donington: Shaun Tyas.

Taylor, S. et al. (2020). *The Place-names of Clackmannanshire*. Donington: Shaun Tyas.

Taylor, S. & Márkus, G. (2010). *Fife Place-name Data*. Retrieved February 2019, from Fife Place-name Data: fife-placenames.glasgow.ac.uk/

Taylor, S. & Markus, G. (2012). *The Place-Names of Fife: Volume Five - Discussion, Glossaries and Edited Texts* (Vol. 5). Donington: Shaun Tyas

Thomas, C. F. (1882). On Islay Place-names. *Proceedings of the Society of Antiquaries of Scotland*, 16, 241–76

Thomson, J. (1832). *John Thomson's Atlas of Scotland*. Retrieved from maps.nls. uk/atlas/thomson/453.html

Tobar an Dualchais (2020). Retrieved from tobarandualchais.co.uk/en/fullrecord/84089/20

Townsend, B. (2015). *Scotch Missed: The Original Guide to the Lost Distilleries of Scotland*. Neil Wilson

University of Copenhagen. (2020). *kirkjuvágr*. Retrieved from ONP: Dictionary of Old Norse Prose: http://onp.ku.dk/onp/onp.php?c370630

Wade-Evans, A. W. (1944). *Vitae Sanctorum Britanniae et Genealogiae*. University of Wales Press Board.

Watson, A. & Allan, E. (1984). *The Place Names of Upper Deeside*. Aberdeen: Aberdeen University Press.

Watson, A. (1995). *The Ochils: Placenames, History, Tradition*. Perth and Kinross District Libraries.

Watson, A. (2013). *Place Names in Much of North-east Scotland*. Rothersthorpe: Paragon Publishing.

Watson, W. J. (1903). *Topographical Notes:* (University of Edinburgh: MS Coll-97/CW9).

Watson, W. J. (1904). *The Place-names of Ross and Cromarty*. Inverness: Northern Counties Printing and Publishing Company

Watson, W. J. (1906). Some Sutherland Names of Places. *The Celtic Review*, 2(8), 360–8.

Watson, W. J. (1922). Classical Gaelic poetry of Panegyric in Scotland. *Transactions of the Gaelic Society of Inverness, 29,* 194–235.

Watson, W. J. (1926). *The History of the Celtic Place-names of Scotland.* Edinburgh: William Blackwood & Sons ltd

Watson, W. J. (2002). *Scottish Place-name Papers.* Edinburgh: Steve Savage Publishers.

Waugh, D. (1985). *The Place-Names of Six Parishes in Caithness Scotland.* (Unpublished PhD thesis) University of Edinburgh.

Waugh, D. (1987). The Scandinavian Element *Staðir* in Caithness, Orkney and Shetland. *Nomina* (11), 61–74.

Wentworth, R. (2003). *Gaelic Words and Phrases from Wester Ross: Faclan is Abairtean à Ros an Iar.* Glasgow: Bell & Bain Lts.

Whiskypedia (2020). Retrieved from scotchwhisky.com/whiskypedia/

Williamson, M. (1942). *The Non-Celtic Place-Names of the Scottish Border Counties* (Unpublished PhD thesis). University of Edinburgh.

Wodrow, R. (1701). *Names of the Islands in Loch Lomand in Irish & English.* (NLS MS Wod. Lett. Qu. II, f. 10).